D0618481

ESCAPE TO

Tuscany

Photography by Antonio Sferlazzo
Text by Candice Gianetti

Fodor's

FODOR'S TRAVEL PUBLICATIONS, INC.
NEW YORK • TORONTO • LONDON • SYDNEY • AUCKLAND • WWW.FODORS.COM

Escape to Tuscany

ISBN 0-679-00296-0
First Edition

Special Sales

Fodor's Travel Publications are available at special discounts for bulk purchases for sales promotions or premiums. Special editions, including personalized covers, excerpts of existing guides, and corporate imprints, can be created in large quantities for special needs. For more information, contact your local bookseller or Special Markets, Fodor's Travel Publications, 201 E. 50th Street, New York, NY 10022. Inquiries from Canada should be directed to your local Canadian bookseller or sent to Random House of Canada, Ltd., Marketing Dept., 2775 Matheson Boulevard East, Mississauga, Ontario L4W 4P7. Inquiries from the United Kingdom should be sent to Fodor's Travel Publications, 20 Vauxhall Bridge Road, London, England SW1V 2SA.

PRINTED IN THE UNITED STATES OF AMERICA
10 9 8 7 6 5 4 3 2 1

Library of Congress Cataloging-in-Publication Data available upon request.

Acknowledgments

From Antonio Sferlazzo: *Mille grazie* Fabrizio. And thanks, Mims, companion of my journey.

From Candice Gianetti: With endless gratitude to Fabrizio La Rocca. Heartfelt thanks and love to three friends whose support was particularly appreciated during the making of this book: Ellen Browne, Phil Wissell, and Joan Warner. For their very practical support, many thanks to Kemwell Holiday Autos, to Marta Marie Lotti at Alitalia, Italy's national airline, and to Mary Kay Hartley at the Italian Government Tourist Office in New York.

Credits

Creative Director and Series Editor: Fabrizio La Rocca
Editorial Director: Karen Cure
Art Director: Tigist Getachew

Editorial Production: Tom Holton
Production/Manufacturing: C. R. Bloodgood, Robert B. Shields
Maps: David Lindroth
Palio photos pp. 72, 75: © Foto Lenzini

Most books on travel shelves are either long on the nitty gritty and short on evocative pictures, or the other way around. We at Fodor's think that the balance in this slim volume is just perfect, rather like the intersection of the most luscious magazine article and a sensible, down-to-earth guidebook. On the road, the useful pages at the end of the book are practically all you need. For the planning, roam through the color photographs up front: Each one reveals a key facet of the corner of Tuscany it portrays, and taken together with the lyrical accompanying text, all convey a sense of place that will take you there before you go. Each page opens up one of Tuscany's most exceptional experiences; each spread leads you to the quintessential places that highlight the spirit of Tuscany at its purest.

Some of these Tuscan adventures are sure to beckon. You may yearn to sojourn amid olive groves and vineyards, to join the harvest and savor aromas of loamy earth and good food. Scramble through quarries whose marble inspired Michelangelo. Learn to make fresh pasta in a cooking school presided over by a Medici descendant. Discover an amazing islet in the Tyrrhenian Sea and sybaritic hot springs known since the days of myth. Take in Florentine fireworks or folkloric rites of spring, horse races or a classic-car race. At day's end, you can seek shelter in crenellated abbeys, castles, and monasteries, Renaissance villas, restored mills, and medieval towers.

While working with words to capture the Tuscan magic that Antonio Sferlazzo defines so beautifully in images, author Candice Gianetti was reminded once again of the truth of the statement that Italians truly know how to live; she rediscovered the pleasures of eating food fresh from the market at the edge of a vineyard under a tree in the hot sun, and was restored by the peace and ineffable beauty of the Tuscan countryside.

It has happened to centuries of travelers before her, and it will happen to you. So be prepared to embrace *il dolce far niente*–the sweetness of doing nothing. Leave your laptop behind. And escape to Tuscany. You owe it to yourself.

–The Editors

AT THE END OF A LONG, TWISTING WHITE ROAD, THE *CASTELLO* OF RIPA D'ÓRCIA suddenly rises up before you, majestic, solid, yet magical. Set on a low hill ringed by dark cypresses that contrast, in classic Tuscan perfection, with the emerald trees and fields that surround them, this fantasy in gray and golden stone seems to float above a sea of green. At the gate, park your steed and pass through a portal into the Middle Ages. Beyond the romantically crenellated manor house where the owners' family has lived since 1438, a church and bell tower and simple stone cottages (now guest quarters) hint of the bustling 13th-century village of shepherds, bakers, carpenters, and others who kept the once-vast estate going. Climbing to the parapet of the fortification walls, testament to the wars that swept the area for centuries, you'll want to volunteer for permanent sentinel duty, for the view is guaranteed to take your breath away. Far below and all around you, the valley stretches out endlessly in a 360-degree panorama: fields burgeoning with wheat, olives, and grapes, dense woods sheltering deer and wild boar, and, winding through it all, the river Órcia. Returning from your next campaign—a two-hour hike to the ancient spa town of Bagno Vignoni, ending in a swim in a steaming pale aqua pool—head for your room terrace for a last look over your domain. As the golden late afternoon fades to black and the sky fills with stars, a sprinkling of lights from a hamlet across the valley pricks the darkness below, and the moon turns the river into a ribbon of quicksilver. The serenity of the place seeps into your soul, and for now you too are at peace, safe within castle walls.

Keys to the Castle

RIPA D'ÓRCIA, VAL D'ÓRCIA, CRETE SENESI

Abandoned by city-bound villagers in the 1950s, the castle still safeguards its owners, descendants of the pope who built nearby Pienza five centuries ago.

St. Catherine of Siena took the healing waters of Bagno Vignoni, as did Lorenzo the Magnificent, whose family turned the town square into an elegant bathing pool.

IN THE WOODED VALLEY FAR BELOW, LIKE SOMETHING OUT OF *CAMELOT,* A LINE of brightly burning torches weaves its way through the black night toward the citadel. Revisiting a centuries-old ritual, young people in monkish sackcloth carrying flaming reed bundles emerge from the high-walled Via Cava di San Giuseppe, one of many mysterious "sunken roads" carved out of the soft rock here by the Etruscans, and walk an old path through the dead fields of winter. As they near the steep-sided outcrop of volcanic rock from which Pitigliano seems to grow, a thing organic and strange, its green mantle of hanging gardens and webbing of Etruscan caves for now veiled in darkness, their chants begin to be heard: "Viva San Giuseppe! Viva San Giuseppe!"—for this is the saint's feast day. Gathered in perfectly preserved medieval and Renaissance piazzas, under the arches of a grand

Rite of Spring

LA TORCIATA DI SAN GIUSEPPE, PITIGLIANO, MAREMMA

The Etruscans built a stronghold on a rock formed when molten ash from a prehistoric volcano shot out of Lake Bolsena at 100 miles an hour, landed here, cooled, and compacted.

Medicean aqueduct, and at windows in the jumble of houses perched on the precipice, the townspeople watch as the youths finally ascend a stone stairway that climbs the rockface. Passing under the now drawbridgeless town gate, they break into an excited run around a man-shaped effigy of reeds as the torches they hold aloft illuminate the honey-colored stone of the square and scatter showers of sparks. At last, chanting wildly as they complete a pagan rite of spring, they toss their torches at the foot of the effigy, igniting a blaze that will symbolically burn away the winter. The square erupts into singing, dancing, and feasting on traditional local pastries as the bonfire slowly dies, leaving a pile of ashes that will be gathered by the women—a token of good luck for the season of rebirth and renewal they have just ushered in.

WHAT SAND IS TO THE SAHARA, OLIVE TREES ARE TO TUSCANY—EVERYWHERE you look, there they are. Planted in neat rows on terraced hillsides, they are always earthily beautiful, but when a breeze riffling through a field exposes the slender, deep green leaves' undersides in an audible shiver of silver, they approach the ethereal. They are said, in fact, to be a gift of the gods—whether Athena, who won Athens' allegiance by conjuring one on the Acropolis, or Hercules, whose olive staff put down roots wherever it touched as he wandered the Mediterranean. Across the region, the best olive oil in the world perfumes virtually every dish, for it is the heart of Tuscan cuisine. It is also a passion bordering on a religion. Anyone with a patch of dirt big enough for a tree prides himself on making his own oil, by laborious, age-old techniques that guarantee liquid gold.

Nectar of the Gods

FATTORIA IL MILIONE DI BRANDIMARTE GUSCELLI, NEAR FLORENCE

Fruity or nutty, flowery or spicy, gold or pale green or deep olive, Tuscan oil is as distinctive as the hand that fashions it.

You'll never complain of high prices again once you've participated in a traditional harvest at Fattoria Il Milione. As throughout Tuscany, for extra-virgin oil (less than 1% acidity), the fruits are not allowed to fall to earth naturally but are picked by hand; combs drawn through the branches rain a mix of bright green olives just starting to ripen and fully mature eggplanty black ones onto orange mesh nets laid on the ground and moved from tree to tree. As the olives are rushed to the *frantoio* for pressing, pungent aromas of fresh oil begin to waft back to the fields, tempting you to press your own to take home. After all your hard work, you'll be ready for the festive communal dinner created from the farm's own fruits, vegetables, meats, wines—and, of course, *olio nuovo:* new oil, green and peppery and smelling of new-mown grass. Divine.

Picking olives is precarious business–and so is growing them. A devastating frost in 1985 killed off almost all the olive trees in Tuscany.

PULLING INTO GIGLIO ISLAND'S HARBOR, TRADE THE FERRY FOR YOUR WAITING water taxi and you're off on an odyssey of enchantment. As you leave the port behind in a wake of sea spray, wild rocky coves and deserted sand beaches call to you like sirens, but strap yourself to the mast and save them for another day. Twenty minutes later, the boatman hands you out onto the dock of a tiny inlet and waves goodbye. Stow your bags in the open-air dumbwaiter, then head up a cliffside path strewn with cactuses and pink-flowering succulents as the salt breeze cools your brow. At the top, a terrace perches at the edge of the world, ringed by the azure expanse of the Tyrrhenian Sea. You have officially arrived in paradise, otherwise known as Pardini's Hermitage. Set like an aerie on a remote granite outcrop, it is reachable only by boat or by foot, along trails through the

An Enchanted Isle

PARDINI'S HERMITAGE, GIGLIO ISLAND, MAREMMA

Giglio is a feast for the senses: Soft breezes scented with mint and myrtle, lavender and broom; silence broken only by birdsong, riffling leaves, and lapping waves. And the raw beauty of earth, sea, and sky.

dense Mediterranean *macchia* that covers most of the 8-square-mile island. Or by donkey—owner Ghigo Pardini lovingly tends 20 of them on the stony terraced hillside behind the vegetable garden, along with goats, sheep, pigs, you name it. Gulls wheel and soar above the path that skirts the coast en route to a lighthouse. Giglio Castello, the fortified medieval town, beckons across luxuriant scrubland—incredible in spring, intensely perfumed with aromatic herbs and ablaze with the most diverse profusion of wildflowers imaginable. Like a guest at a country-house party, you'll wander in and out of Pardini's, returning from excursions to swim, read on your own ocean-view patio, or wander from viewpoint to soul-filling viewpoint, joining fellow guests at night for dinner and conversation. On Calypso's perfect island, Odysseus longed for home. You'll want to stay forever.

Giglio was named for the goats that once roamed in abundance. Today you're more likely to spot one of Ghigo's donkeys clambering along the rocks—or an even more elusive mammal here, identified by its paintbrush, its Pentax, or its pair of shades.

A LITTLE MOVIE MAGIC HELPED TURN SANT'ANNA IN Camprena into the ruined monastery with the "unoccupied, gone-to-seed feeling" the director of *The English Patient* says he wanted for the dying pilot and his heartsick nurse, Hana. But today, in the 14th-century former Benedictine abbey, set amid fields of olives and cypresses, the mood lingers. Though open to overnight guests, the place often seems deserted as the few staff members tend the farm or disappear somewhere down the stark white corridors. So much easier, then, to wander through the film fantasy. Here a door leads to the small *chiostro*, centered by an antique well, where Hana played hopscotch. Another opens onto a much civilized version of the wild garden where the Indian officer

An Abandoned Monastery

SANT'ANNA IN CAMPRENA, NEAR PIENZA, CRETE SENESI

Footsteps on the cotto floor echo across the empty spaces of Sant'Anna's long-parishless church, renovated in the 17th century.

pitched his tent, with the circular pool—now ringed with potted lemon trees—that the patient was danced around to celebrate the end of the war. Best of all is the refectory, frescoed in 1503 by Il Sodoma with scenes from the life of Christ, that was the model for the dying man's bedchamber. Take a seat on the bench and, like the only visitor in a museum, savor the details at your leisure—the harbor scene with tiny boats, the architectural set pieces, Sodoma's signature little dogs. When night falls, the smells of traditional Tuscan cooking and the babble of guests in the dining room briefly bring the place to life. But as you settle in to sleep, enveloped in the silence of the isolated setting, it's easy to drift back into the fantasy and imagine yourself indeed alone, a trespasser in a place time has left behind.

MENDACES OSTENDIT
QUI MACULAVERUNT ILLUM
SAPIENTIAE CAP. 10 N. 17

SIGN UP FOR TEMPORARY MEMBERSHIP IN THE FIORONI FAMILY, AND THEY'LL let you in on a ritual nearly as old as the Tuscan hills: the *vendemmia*, harvest time in the vineyards. At Poggio Alloro, their farm in the Val d'Elsa—as indeed all over Italy, where more grapes are transfigured into wine than anywhere else on earth—these are long but happy days, the culmination of a year's work, worry, and wait. At the perfect moment, when the gold and ruby fruits have just enough sweetness and not too much acid, they are picked by family, friends, and other recruits, who sing and laugh in the clear, golden light of autumn as they move quickly down the neat rows of vines to thwart the first frost. The pale grapes are the stuff of Tuscany's best white wine, the straw-colored Vernaccia di San Gimignano, produced only in the

A Harvest Home

POGGIO ALLORO, NEAR SAN GIMIGNANO

vicinity of the "Town of the Beautiful Towers," which rises up like the Emerald City on a hill beyond the fields. The red are destined to become Chianti Colli Senesi, chianti of the Sienese hills, where somehow things remain more steadfastly Italian than in neighboring "Chiantishire." At dinner around a communal table, vintages from past years will be liberally poured by your gentle and charming host, Amico, one of three brothers who own the farm, to complement a meal prepared by the Fioroni mothers. If you're lucky, *bistecca alla fiorentina*—a huge slab of steak made from the much prized white Chianina cattle—will be on the menu. As the meat, brushed lightly with olive oil, is grilled outdoors over a wood fire, the rich scents waft to the heavens in a burnt offering to the god Bacchus, heartfelt thanks for his glorious gift of wine.

The grapes may no longer be stomped by foot, but they're still picked by hand, one sun-kissed bunch at a time.

ONE LOOK AT THE SIMPLE BEAUTY OF VIGNAMAGGIO'S Renaissance villa and garden, and—like the wedding party in Kenneth Branagh's *Much Ado About Nothing,* which was filmed here—you too may feel like dancing for joy amid the topiary. "Harmony of the parts" was the age's standard of beauty, and nothing could be more harmonious than the gentle, virtually unembellished façade, its soft pink plaster weathered in places to patches of gold. Under a sundial painted onto the wall, statues wreathed in roses flank the pointed Gothic arch door like festively adorned pages eternally waiting to welcome their mistress home. Off the terrace, lined with clay pots sprouting lemon trees, is the small, sweet garden, with neat boxwood-edged quadrants and

Mona Lisa Slept Here

VILLA VIGNAMAGGIO, GREVE IN CHIANTI

In June, roses perfume the air, while the heat of summer releases the tangy scent of potted lemons, the herbal intensity of lavender, and the sultry note of jasmine.

sculpted bushes, fragrant jasmine and lavender climbing an old stone wall, a shady allée, and a riotous tangle of wild roses down a mossy path. Lisa Gherardini, Leonardo's model for the *Mona Lisa*, was born here in 1479, and though you can't sleep in her room, a few others are available in the still mostly private residence. Ask for a tour of the cellars where wine has been made for centuries—the name Vignamaggio comes from the vines that carpet the hills in green each May, twining away between silver-leafed olives and spiky cypresses. Awaiting her swain's return from the wars, Emma Thompson's Beatrice perches in an olive tree reciting poetry; you can brush up on your Shakespeare (or Dante) from a seat by the pool. Each time you glance up at the quintessential Chianti tableau before you, your smile will rival the most famous one in history.

THOUGH SINNERS IN ITALY ARE NO LONGER REQUIRED TO WEAR SACKCLOTH AS public penance at Lent, power-mad politicians and church-bashing dramatists often find their sins writ large—very large—in papier-mâché. But you don't have to get the jokes to enjoy Viareggio's Carnevale, where do-badders are skewered and social evils decried in sculptural tableaux on gigantic floats. Circling the palm-studded island of this summer resort's beachfront promenade, lined with Deco and Nouveau storefronts and grand hotels, they literally overflow with fiesta-colored paper-and-paste clowns, warlords, musketeers, and monsters straight out of *Where the Wild Things Are*, along with caricatures of well-known faces, sometimes attached to outrageous, anatomically correct naked bodies. These are no Macy's parade floats—they are works of art, created by men who spend

Mardi Gras, Tuscan Style

CARNEVALE, VIAREGGIO, VERSILIA

the rest of the year designing sets for opera and films. As each 35-ton *carro* sails through the sea of merrymakers that surrounds it, everything is in motion: the figures' hands wave, eyes roll, aliens pop out of characters' mouths, a woman's bra rises and falls to reveal rotating breasts. Not to mention the hundred or more costumed humans on each platform who dance and shake pompoms to blaring music. As you dodge confetti, watch for towering figures that seem to have stepped off the floats to walk among the revelers. Should you crave elbow room, catch the parade from four stories up, on the roof terrace of the Palace Hotel, before setting off again for a night of street feasts and fireworks. When it's all over, the winning *carri* will go on display for a year, then rest in pieces in the workshops where they were born, one alien head and monster fang at a time.

A typical float's 32 wheels carry 400 pounds of glue, 2,000 pounds of newspapers, 800 pounds of paint, 4,000 pounds of clay, some wood, a little iron... and a lot of people.

CHE MALE VI FO'

"Bevete più Latte" ("Drink more milk"), the float with the buxom miss, was a heartfelt plea for politicians to nourish themselves and grow.

ARISE FROM SWEET DREAMS INSPIRED BY THE TWINKLING MOTHER OF PEARL scattered across your antique bedstead to survey a dreamily idyllic landscape from the window of a 13th-century tower. An austere stone sentinel at the end of its own white road, La Torre stands solitary and remote amid fields painted in the richest earth tones on an artist's palette, from the dark burnt umber of freshly plowed furrows to the spun-gold yellow ochre of wheat ready for harvesting. Here as throughout the Crete, south of Siena—a place of lunar hills of bare white clay topped with a tonsure of grass and trees, softly undulating farmland like a vast lumpy bed with a velvet spread, and jagged cliffs of white limestone clutched by blazing yellow broom—the hands of man and nature collaborate to create of the earth itself an artwork of ever changing form, texture, and color.

The Art of the Landscape

AGRITURISMO LA TORRE, NEAR PIENZA, CRETE SENESI

Is it coincidence that so many earth colors in the world's paintboxes—terra-cotta, burnt sienna, Tuscan red—have Italian names?

Lay a picnic cloth on the lawn and watch the play of light across a rippling canvas of spring green *grano duro* (pasta wheat) and, behind it, in a pasture at the foot of oak-mantled hills, a flock of white sheep placed with painterly perfection. Scan right and the green melts into a patch of pale pink blossoms as your eyes are drawn inexorably to the dark cone of Monte Amiata in the distance, ominously evoking the volcano it once was. A thin, dark line of cypresses, like a column of advancing soldiers, stretches for miles along the road to Radicofani, whose hilltop *rocca* (citadel) was the next link in a chain of medieval signal towers. More modern signals will guide you home at night to your private fortress: tiny white Christmas lights draped from its four very solid corners.

FOLLOW THE RIVER SERCHIO UP FROM Lucca along the Garfagnana, the narrow soft green valley between the jagged white marble peaks of the Apuan Alps and the chestnut-covered slopes of the Apennines. After about 40 miles, you'll arrive at Mulin del Rancone, a century-old mill that has traded in its grindstones for guestrooms. The rustic stone *mulino* was built right on the river—here, a rocky-bedded stream—smack against a huge vine-draped cone of lava, like an arrowhead jabbed through the streambed by some testy chthonic giant. Across the water, hillsides blossom with clusters of dark evergreens, a red-roofed hamlet, and a ruined medieval fortress on a high crest with a view of both mountain ranges.

By the Old Mill Stream

MULIN DEL RANCONE, CAMPORGIANO, GARFAGNANA

Gabriele Bertucci, who runs the place, is an ambassador of Garfagnana cooking abroad but plugs away at home as well—starting with his 3-year-old.

Ride there on one of the horses grazing in the inn's pasture, or stay close and fish for trout in the clear stream, watch for elusive gray herons, or paddle around the shallow pool created with rock dams each summer. Sip a Campari on the terrace as the sun sinks behind the mountains, then settle into the homey dining room, where real Garfagnana mothers cook for you what their mothers and grandmothers before them made for their families, starting with the region's two essentials: *farro* (spelt), used in soups and pastas, and *castagne* (chestnuts), used as flour to make bread, polenta, cakes, and pancakes. In your room, throw the window open and fall asleep to the sound of water rushing over rocks as it journeys to the sea. Somewhere downstream a miller will rise with the dawn to grind chestnuts into the stuff of tradition—and of breakfast.

Where Sky Melts into Sea

TORRE LE CANNELLE, NEAR TALAMONE, MAREMMA

IN AN ISOLATED STONE TOWER HIGH ABOVE THE SEA, WHERE ONCE LOOKOUTS KEPT WATCH for Barbary pirates, sit within a circle of glass walls and revel in one of nature's everyday miracles in a far-from-everyday setting. Surrounded by 5,000 pristine acres of woods and the sound of wind blowing right through the panes, settle in as a wash of colors deepening from soft pinks and lavenders to intense oranges and fiery reds spills down into the sea with the sun, casting into increasing silhouette a string of islands said to be peaks of a drowned continent or, more poetically, pearls dropped from Venus' necklace. Framed by the arcs of wooded headlands—Monte Argentario peninsula to the south and Piombino to the north—they sit like stepping stones across the horizon: rocky Giglio, its little sister Giannutri, Dumas' Montecristo, and fish-shaped Elba, Napoleon's mountainous refuge. Once the great star has gone dark, the lesser ones

While moon-gazing at Cala di Forno, a local girl was carried off by the pirate Barbarossa to Constantinople, to the harem of the sultan Suleyman.

begin twinkling all around your penthouse observatory. In the light of day, watch for wild boar as you appreciate the view east, over the woods and wheat fields of inland Maremma, then head out for a gallop along the shore. Arrange for a boatman to pick you up at your private beach for day of fishing, or head off with him for a tour of the coast, stopping for a swim at an idyllic cove like Cala di Forno, an old smuggler's hideout, or a peek into grottoes in a group of rocks that emerge out of the crystal clear water. Cruising by the adjacent Regional Park of the Maremma, you'll spy six other towers that relayed messages up and down the coast for centuries, warning of the return of the foreign marauders each summer, kind of like tourists with very bad manners.

AT THE END OF A LONG DRIVE EDGED IN cypresses, a vaulted arch of soft rose brick topped by a 13th-century tower is your gateway into the very romantic world of the Locanda dell'Amorosa, the Inn of the Amorous. Fitted gently into a hamlet where owners and workers of the surrounding farm once lived side by side, the inn centers on a piazza ringed with evidence of seven centuries of life, from a medieval well to a church in Renaissance dress to an 18th-century manor with shell-shaped staircase. Cupid has been busy here, for everywhere you look he's strewn flowers. Tiny-petaled pink geraniums spill lavishly from windowboxes beneath the upper arches of a graceful double portico grafted onto the former

Love in Bloom

LOCANDA DELL'AMOROSA, NEAR SINALUNGA, CRETE SENESI

A long lover's lane of cypresses leads to this inn, crafted from what was once a village of 250 souls—and an exorcist.

stables. Throughout the village, roses of red, orange, bright pink, and salmon cling to walls whose long history is written in patchings of stone, brick, and plaster. In spring, purple wisteria dripping from a pergola fills the air with its heady perfume. Stroll the old paths arm in arm, pausing in the garden to pick rosemary for remembrance and marjoram, herb of Aphrodite, then watch the sun set over fields of vines and olives, wheat and sunflowers. When the bell tower chimes the dinner hour, head for the intimate restaurant, created around the rustic brick walls and arches of the old stables, where a pool of soft light that seems to envelop your table alone sets the stage for a meal in which every morsel is an aphrodisiac. Returning to your room with some Tuscan sparkling wine, light a fire in the hearth, and your perfect day is headed for its amorously perfect end.

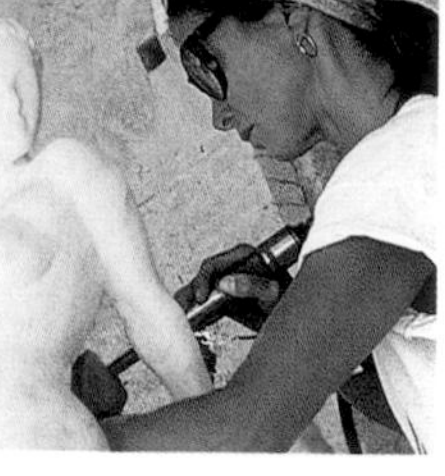

WALK IN MICHELANGELO'S FOOTSTEPS THROUGH the quarries of Carrara, where spinning cables studded with diamonds slice out of the mountainsides the purest white statuary marble in the world. The sculptor came here to supervise the cutting of his blocks, and if you stare hard at those scattered about today, you too may see Davids and Madonnas struggling to get out. On work days, the air is filled with the echoing whir of flywheels and the grinding of trucks zigzagging their vertiginous way from hairpin to hairpin on the narrow roads, delivering future museum pieces to the docks at nearby Marina di Carrara. But on a Sunday, as you follow hiking trails blazed in slashes of paint, the only sound is the crunch of your boots on the scree that flows down into the

Into the Marble Mountains

THE QUARRIES OF CARRARA, APUAN ALPS

valley like a blindingly white river. Wandering this wonderland of dust, which coats every wildflower and blade of grass, you come across a beach of it, complete with pooled water with nowhere to go and a convenient slab to catch some rays on. Climb on past vast amphitheaters of cut rock tiers and spiral staircases for giants till you reach Campocecina, a grassy plateau at the top of this alpine world. The view couldn't be more spectacular: Beyond the bowl of mountains—their exposed flesh of metamorphic limestone alternating with bands of forest—urban Carrara spills from the foothills to the sea, a scant few miles away. On a clear day you can see the coast almost to the Cinque Terre and south to Livorno. At sundown, stop at a rustic *rifugio* for a hearty dinner, some trail talk with fellow hikers, and a warm, dustless bed.

"Oh, cursed be the day and the hour that I left Carrara," Michelangelo wrote when forced by his patron to get his marble elsewhere.

Some bemoan the destruction quarrying has wrought on the craggy Apuan Alps, but few who have walked among them can deny their strange and stirring beauty.

ENTER THE FORESTS OF THE CASENTINO, CLOAKING A SHARP APENNINE RIDGE an hour east of Florence, and experience the deep stillness and mystical beauty that have drawn spiritual seekers for a thousand years. In 1012, St. Romualdo built his hermitage here, and for eight centuries the brothers of Camaldoli made it their sacred duty to nurture the forest and thus their seclusion. Witness the results on a drive through miles of towering silver firs whose branches, like arms upraised in prayer, let only thin shafts of light penetrate, ending at the wrought-iron gate that separates the *eremo* from the world. Here each hermit lives, solitary and silent, in an austere cottage with a walled garden, emerging for Mass in the surprisingly Baroque church outside the gate draped, ghostlike, in Benedictine white robe and hood. Breathtaking vistas slow your progress to La

A Forest of Mysteries

LA VERNA AND CAMALDOLI MONASTERIES, THE CASENTINO

The Casentino—as poet Gabriele D'Annunzio called it, a "land of passion and of prayer." La Verna, high on its rock, has been compared to the ark stranded atop Ararat.

Verna, a monastery perched dramatically atop a limestone outcrop, where in 1224 St. Francis received the first stigmata. Visit the church and chapels, adorned with 15 Della Robbia masterpieces donated by the faithful; wander the mossy ravines and rock caves where Francis meditated and slept; pause as the brown-robed monks process, with medieval chants, to the basilica; or walk through intensely quiet woods to the top of Monte Penna to take in lonely, mist-shrouded views of the valley far below. A major pilgrimage site through the ages, La Verna has a long tradition of welcoming overnight guests. At dinner, you may find yourself discussing theology with a German nun on retreat, or the ecstasy of nature with a pagan. Whatever your persuasion, you'll not leave this forest of mysteries with your spirit untouched.

OUT OF A CRACK IN THE EARTH, INTO A VOLCANIC CRATER WITH WALLS OF CLAY, up through layers of mineral-rich sediment and algae into a vast pool of crystal blue, the healing hot spring of Saturnia surges at 160 gallons per second—as it has for 3,000 years at least. Myth tells us that Saturn, in a fit of divine anger, created it with a lightning bolt to calm the constantly feuding mortals. The Etruscans, whose tombs and cyclopean walls are strewn all over this part of the Maremma, considered the spring sacred. Roman legions returning home on the Via Clodia—whose paving stones are still visible under the town's Roman gate—stopped to soothe their battle-weary bodies in it. Today, as you glide through the exactly 98.6-degree sulfurous brew bubbling up around you, your face enveloped in a cloud of warm mist and every square inch of skin tingling, you

Taking the Waters

TERME DI SATURNIA, MAREMMA

Pleasure and peace seem bonded inextricably to the warm, sulfurous mist that surrounds you.

know no Caesar ever had it so good. Now the centerpiece of a luxurious spa, the spring has evolved into a kind of therapeutic water park, with cascades ranging from a fireplug-force torrent that pummels the knots out of your neck to a streaming, mushroom-shaped fountain just for fun. As you wander about in a white terry robe, venture in and out of the pool in between being slathered with thermal mud and punching an 80-pound sack in an aerobic boxing class. At dawn, take a short walk past farmland and pasturing horses to a steamy spot where overflow from the spa rushes headlong down a hillside, sculpting ice-blue pools from terraces of white volcanic rock. Alone amid velvety green fields and a rocky, reed-fringed stream, take your pick of natural hot tubs, lie back, and feel your bones melt away.

The architecture of well-being, as the spa defines it, consists of materials in tune with their environment, flowing water, and round shapes for it to pass through, collecting dynamic energy as it goes and transfering that energy to those who bask in it.

WHEN 13TH-CENTURY WAYFARERS APPROACHED San Gimignano on the Via Francigena, the pilgrimage route between Canterbury and Rome, they saw a city bristling with 72 stone towers, each a clan fortress with family homes clustered at its feet. While not a unique sight in feud-racked Tuscany—Florence once had 200 towers, many over 200 feet tall—it did earn San Gimignano the epithet "City of the Beautiful Towers." Most of the structures have since crumbled on their foundations, but the 14 that remain give a vivid sense of life in a world where power and prestige were translated into pillars of stone, and where at any moment you might need to seek refuge from an attack by your next-door neighbors—or rain rocks or boiling pitch onto their heads yourself. Set your

City of Towers

HOTEL LA CISTERNA, SAN GIMIGNANO

God *is* in the details—in San Gimignano, a stone cross of the Knights of Malta, a rose window in brick, Ghirlandaio frescoes honoring a child saint.

watch back to the Middle Ages, and enter one of three remaining gates in the town walls. Within you'll find the medieval city almost intact, few concessions made to the passage of time. At its heart is the former Duomo, frescoed floor to ceiling with wonderfully detailed Biblical scenes, including a hell gruesome enough to scare any poor pilgrim back onto the path of virtue. Wander narrow streets lined with Romanesque and Gothic architecture from prosperous silk-trading days, then climb the Torre Grossa for a panoramic view of the vineyards and fields of the Val d'Elsa. Later, head back to your hotel on the *palazzo*-rimmed Piazza della Cisterna, with its 13th-century well, and retire to your flower-decked terrace. Over a bottle of the esteemed Vernaccia, enjoy your view of the valley, a jumble of clay-pot roofs, and at least seven towers—but watch out for flying rocks.

CROWNING A PEAK THAT DROPS DRAMATICALLY DOWN through a forest of cypresses to steep gorges and low hills of bare rock, Monte Oliveto Maggiore stands majestically amid a whispering of olives. In 1319 a nobleman-turned-ascetic had a vision of monks climbing a silver stairway to heaven from this place, where he'd lived for years as a hermit, and so he built a church and founded an abbey here. Today's monks continue to live according to the Benedictine Rule, combining prayer, work, and study, and tending to the modern-day pilgrims who come to pray and to marvel at the extraordinary High Renaissance fresco cycle that rings the Great Cloister. In 36 panels of color and movement, reverence and exuberance, devils and saints and fallen women, two artists tell stories from the life of

Stairway to Heaven

MONTE OLIVETO MAGGIORE, CRETE SENESI

The brothers wear white robes in honor of the Virgin, whose Della Robbian incarnation welcomes visitors from a niche above the entrance.

St. Benedict, the 6th-century founder of Western monasticism. Luca Signorelli, whose work greatly influenced Michelangelo's Sistine Chapel, painted nine panels; the other 27 are by Il Sodoma, whose figures (especially the young men) exude sensuousness and emotion. If you stay overnight at the guesthouse, you can return again and again to absorb all the details in these and in the elaborately inlaid choir stalls, explore your spirituality in talks with a brother, or spend hours with your own thoughts and nature in walks through the peaceful surrounding woods. Be sure to get back, though, in time for evening vespers, when the Baroque church resonates with Gregorian chant. Afterwards, as you're making friends in the abbey's restaurant, the monks will be in their refectory, dining in silent contemplation, feet resting gently on a stair of silver.

AS SCENTS OF JASMINE AND ROSES WAFT BY YOUR POOLSIDE CHAISE ON THIS sultry Tuscan day, you reach for a sip of frothy iced cappuccino, then lie back to drink in something even better: a miraculous bird's-eye view of one of the world's most fabulous cities. For below your secluded perch atop leafy Bellosguardo—named "beautiful hill" by the friend of Dante's who built his *torre* (now your charmingly atmospheric inn) here in the 14th century—the treasure house of art and architecture that is Florence lies spread out like a carpet of soft red and gold at your bare feet. At dead center of the tapestry, formed by a rosy sprawl of terra-cotta-roofed houses punctuated by spired churches and ringed by low green hills, rises the ultimate symbol of this city where the Renaissance was born: the Duomo, with its vast, graceful cupola that, in Emerson's words, seems "set down

A Pool with a View

TORRE DI BELLOSGUARDO, FLORENCE

If the glory of Giotto's campanile fills you, as it did Ruskin, with "wild, sickening yearning—the desire of the moth for the star," recuperate at your hilltop aerie—and wait for nightfall.

like an archangel's tent in the midst of the city." Beside this masterwork of Brunelleschi, completed in 1436 and still the largest unsupported dome in Europe, Giotto's multicolor-marble campanile of a century earlier stands straight and tall in all its Gothic glory. This view, virtually unchanged since well before adoptive Florentines Robert and Elizabeth Barrett Browning began making the 20-minute walk from town to take it in, inspired her to write these lines: "From Tuscan Bellosguardo... where Galileo stood at nights to take/ The vision of the stars, we have found it hard,/ gazing upon the earth and heaven, to make/ A choice of beauty." Looking out from Torre di Bellosguardo's garden today, the choice seems easier, for compared to earth like this, how beautiful could heaven be?

AS THE CREAM-COLORED '54 LANCIA AURELIA COUPE PULLS AWAY TO CHEERS from the church steps, a space-agey '49 Ferrari Uovo in soft metallic blue slides into its place. After a quick conference with timekeepers, the driving team, jaunty in goggles and flowing white scarves, collect their welcoming gifts—a bottle of local wine, a bag of amaretti—and, with waves, smiles, and a jolt of espresso, they're off. So it will go for the next two hours as 360 of the fastest, most elegant classic cars from museums and collectors' garages all over the world pass through this checkpoint in a three-day, thousand-mile rally called the Mille Miglia. Piloting the Bugattis and Maseratis, the Bentleys and Porsches, in all the candy colors and plenty of high-gloss red, the racing champions and enthusiastic amateurs, Euro TV stars and princes, speed from

The Great Road Show

MILLE MIGLIA CLASSIC-CAR ROAD RALLY, VIA CASSIA

Originally run as a flat-out race with an incredible record time of 10 hours, the Mille Miglia is today more a very fast parade.

Brescia to Rome and back, reveling in the pleasure of the countryside and the appreciation of the crowds lining the route. Heading out of the Eternal City on the Via Cassia, the old Roman road, they make their first stop in Tuscany at the hilltop town of Radicofani, whose fortress can be seen for miles rising above a flat plain. Through fields of spring-green wheat, past the stark rockfaces of the Crete, and under the medieval portal of Siena right into the Campo they go, their massed presence quite a sight amid the elegant *palazzi*. Then it's on through the golden Tuscan afternoon past the vineyards and olive groves of Chianti, into Florence's Piazza del Duomo, and across mist-shrouded mountain passes toward the finish line in Lombardy—the end of another edition of the race Enzo Ferrari called "the most beautiful traveling museum in the world."

200
152
324

Riding with the Butteri

AZIENDA REGIONALE AGRICOLA DI ALBERESE, MAREMMA

SADDLE UP AND RIDE OFF INTO THE SUNRISE WITH the *butteri*, the legendary cowboys of Italy's wild west, as they make their rounds to see how the dogies are gittin' along. Every day of the year, come rain, shine, or snow, one of these horsemen mounts his sturdy bay and sets out to make sure that the rare white cattle in his charge—among only a few thousand left in the world—haven't poked their lyre-shaped horns into anything they shouldn't have. If you can hold your seat for four butt-numbing hours, you can tag along with the strong, silent one as he tracks them—practically knowing each by name—across this 10,000-acre Tuscan Ponderosa, which has been owned over the last millennium by Benedictine monks, the Knights of Malta, the granddukes of Lorraine (whose villa can be your home on the range), and now by the region of Tuscany. For your pains, as you traverse open pastures and fields of sunflowers, pick your way carefully among woods of umbrella pine or chase the wind on sandy beaches, you'll be rewarded with glimpses of ruined medieval watchtowers, herons and egrets wading in marshes, ducks paddling in vast drainage canals, and semiwild Maremma horses drinking peacefully from a pool or racing across the plains for the pure joy of it. When the *buttero* breaks into a gallop to round up a stray, you'll get a sample of the skills that once trounced the cowboys of Buffalo Bill's traveling Wild West Show in a challenge match in Rome. For a full helping, come to the August rodeo that commemorates that event with all the roping, prancing, and swirling dust a cowpoke could ask for.

Like the cattle he shepherds, the *buttero* is the last of his breed. At this ranch in the Maremma, both are valued and protected.

There's a deep harmony between the *buttero* and his Maremma horse, a special, hardy breed—long the choice of the Italian army—that is raised here semiwild.

AS THE SETTING SUN GILDS THE PONTE VECCHIO, PAINTING THE river with ripples of molten gold, you gaze in awe until the last pink streaks of sky fade away and night falls over Florence. Tucked in snugly among the crowd on the Ponte Santa Trinità, one bridge down, you wait—along with thousands draped precariously over the high embankment walls and gathered in every window of the antique *palazzi*, shops, and hotels that line the Arno—for the pyrotechnic grand finale of the Feast of San Giovanni (John the Baptist), the city's patron saint. When the streetlights are suddenly extinguished, an expectant hush falls, broken by the hiss of the first rocket shot off from the hillside below the Piazzale Michelangelo. Trailing a glittering wake, it explodes with a bang into a great puffball of color

Baptism of Fire

FIREWORKS, FEAST OF SAN GIOVANNI, FLORENCE

Friendly fire breaks out over Santa Croce's gothic head while in her heart the bones of Galileo and Michelangelo rest in peace.

that lingers in midair for a heartbeat, then dissolves into twinkling tendrils that drift slowly through space, to settle in a fine drizzle on the water's surface, a hint of the Baptist's promised river of fire. Again and again a canopy of stars spills over the Ponte Vecchio, their illumination throwing into bold relief the ancient churches and palaces. In the streets there's an infectious excitement, with old and young in holiday mode simultaneously oohing and jostling for a better look. But if something a bit more intimate is to your taste, the next best thing to being invited to a fireworks party at a contessa's riverfront penthouse is joining an elegant dinner for 30 on the rooftop terrace of the Continental Hotel. As the spectacle draws to a close, raise a champagne glass in a toast to a sparkling night and to the saintly guest of honor, who holds this radiant city in his hands.

WHEN NAPOLEON TIED LUCCA UP WITH A BIG red bow and presented it to his sister Élisa to rule, she scoured the olive-clad hills and found a villa worthy of a *principessa*. She had, after all, a few hundred to choose from—from the 14th-century hunting lodge of Machiavelli's model for *The Prince* to aristocratic residences built in the last days of Lucca's independence as a city-state. Today many can be visited on drives along roads that meander past streams, tiny villages, and old parish churches. Hidden behind high stone walls, guarded by elaborate wrought-iron gates, or reached by a long avenue of cypresses, these testimonials to prosperity and good taste generally follow the austere lines of the Tuscan Renaissance,

La Dolce Vita

THE VILLAS OF THE LUCCAN HILLS

Paganini fiddled for Élisa's guests in the *teatro di verzura* of Villa Reale (opposite, top). Villa Torrigiani's exuberance (below, left) is echoed at Villa Mansi.

but two break out into full-blown Baroque. Lucca's ambassador to the court of Louis XIV brought a bit of Versailles' dazzle to his Tuscan home (now Villa Torrigiani), from the wedding-cake façade studded with classical sculptures to magnificent gardens complete with elaborate crisscrossing stone staircases, fountains, and nymph temples. Even more spectacular are the gardens at Villa Reale, boasting a swan pool worthy of a Sun King and a superb 17th-century "green theater" carved out of boxwood shrubs. If catching a glimpse of this way of life isn't enough, rent out one of these historic gems and live it: Dine alfresco on an elegant triple-arched loggia. Ask the maid to serve lemonade by the flower-rimmed pool overlooking the valley, then sneak off for a game of tennis on the grounds of your 18th-century shooting lodge. The sweet life indeed.

When you've seen the *principessa*'s swan pond and Villa Bernardini's Napoleonic bed, head back to your own aristocratic digs for a more contemporary pleasure: lunch by the pool.

Cooking with Class

THE VILLA TABLE, BADIA A COLTIBUONO, GAIOLE IN CHIANTI

AS YOU WATCH THE PASTA DOUGH BEING ROLLED AND PULLED UNTIL IT reaches the far corners of the table, thin as a whisper but elastic, like a stretched-out balloon, it seems likely that this will be the one thing you won't master this week. The risotto you stir to the point of madness comes out exquisitely. The spinach gnocchi you roll into beautiful little eggs pop up out of the boiling broth like bubbles in a champagne glass. The veal rollatini? Bravissima! Your inspiration and guide during this culinary crash course is Lorenza de' Medici, descendant of the grand dukes, the popes, and—more important this week—author of dozens of cookbooks and star of her own PBS cooking show. Each morning you and your classmates learn to prepare a menu, which you then "evaluate" at lunch, assisted by liberal swigs of wine from her thousand-year-old Chianti estate, Badia a Coltibuono (Abbey of the Good Harvest). After a stroll in the Renaissance garden, scented with lemons and lavender and jasmine, wander the 2,000 acres of woods or cool off in the flower-edged pool before heading out for excursions ranging from the important wine estate Castello di Brolio to a local ceramics workshop. In the evening, as guests of Lorenza's friends, you may dine (and sip) elegantly under the gaze of a Picasso and end the meal with a performance in an antique puppet theater, or take a preprandial tour of villa gardens filmed in Bertolucci's *Stealing Beauty* and of frescoed and gilded rooms untouched since the 18th century. Returning each night to your room, crafted from former monks' cells, you'll feel anything but monastic, sated as you are with good food, new friendships, a little knowledge, and a lot of wine.

Come to the Abbey of the Good Harvest to learn about cooking, "a skill," says Lorenza de' Medici, "that requires, above all, sensory judgments–touching, observing, smelling and tasting."

TWICE EACH SUMMER, SIENA CELEBRATES ITS ILLUSTRIOUS HISTORY WITH ITALY'S most famous festival: the Palio. Begun as a mad dash through the streets in the 11th century, this heart-stopping horse race is today run in the shell-shaped Piazza del Campo but is no less mad. Rife with bribery and intrigue, it is intensely important to the Sienese because its outcome determines the supremacy of one of their 17 *contrade*, or districts—like clubs they're born into and are fiercely loyal to all their lives. Join the crush of spectators at the center of the piazza, or do whatever it takes to snag a precious seat in the grandstands. It will all be worth it the minute you hear the drums and trumpets announce the arrival of 600 or so young men with costumes—and sometimes faces—straight out of a 15th-century painting. For two unforgettable hours they circle the Campo in a stately procession, dressed in brightly colored velvets and ermine, armor and mail, holding shields,

Raw Siena

THE PALIO

swords, crossbows, on foot or mounted on regally caparisoned horses. Then, with a final salute from flagtossers performing routines passed down from knightly traditions, the last of the cortege exits, silence falls, and the tension becomes almost unbearable. Suddenly an explosive crack is heard, and the horses thunder off on the dirt track created for the occasion, edged at the dangerous turnings with a wall of mattresses to cushion the horses and jockeys who crash against them. Three times around—a total of about 90 seconds—and it's over. Hysteria ensues. Wildly crying, screaming, and hugging one another, members of the *contrada* with the winning horse race to church with the *palio,* the silk trophy banner for which the race is named, to sing a Te Deum in thanks before setting out on a night of joyous carousing. Today the are the champions of their world.

Brave, bareback, and bribable: From the Maremma, Sardinia, and the Roman plains, jockeys come to make their fortune.

The *sbandierata*, or ritual flag waving, is at once an invocation of victory and a salute to the *contrada*.

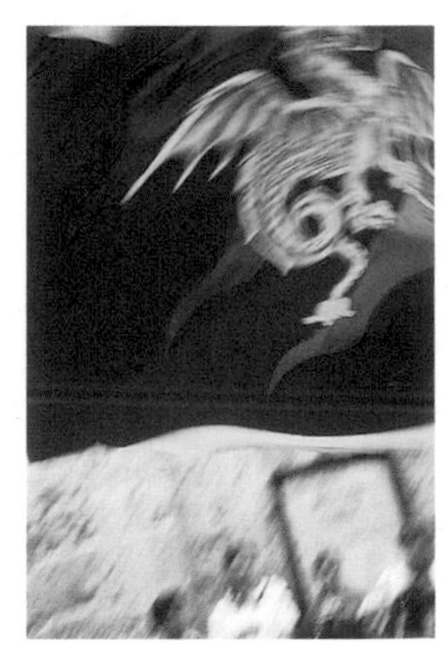

CUT LOOSE FROM TERRA FIRMA AND GO WHERE THE wind takes you as you float over the postcard landscapes of Tuscany in a bright red balloon. Snug in your wicker basket like a bottle of Chianti, lift off in the soft light of dawn and watch the *castello* and ancient city walls of Rapolano Terme slowly zoom down to Lego size as you ascend. Silently, motionlessly, as though it were standing still and the earth gently slipping by below, the balloon chases its shadow across fields ripe with grain or furrowed like chocolate-brown corduroy, the only sound the dull roar of the propane burner warming the air in the nylon envelope. As you glide over the strange, bumpy surface of the Crete, prepare for wonderful surprises—an isolated farmhouse atop a rocky ridge; deer or wild

Up, Up, and Away

BALLOONING IN TUSCANY, RAPOLANO TERME, CRETE SENESI

From the air, it's easier to get the lay of the land—how cities developed, valleys interconnect, rivers meander.

boar in a clearing, or a flock of grazing sheep; low hills with exposed limestone on one flank, woods on the other, spilling down to a perfect little lake into which the sky has poured its blue. Soar to 3,000 feet for an eagle's-eye view of medieval urban planning, snatch a souvenir as you sail through the treetops, or skim a field of golden sunflowers just inches above their nodding heads. Outside Montepulciano's walls, dip down for a visit with a farmer as you hover over a vineyard dripping with fruits fated to become the elegant Vino Nobile. Back on the ground, hoist a glass of champagne in the traditional "Survivors' Toast." Before snuggling into bed at night at your B&B in Rapolano—a spa town known for its sulfurous thermal baths—brush your teeth with bubbling spring water from the tap, crowning the day's aerial wonders with one straight out of the earth.

JUST OUTSIDE RADDA IN CHIANTI, TURN ONTO A narrow road edged in lacy walls of sunny yellow broom so intoxicatingly fragrant you'll want to fill the car with it. Wind your way up through grapevines and olive trees that spill down to the horizon in all directions, then negotiate a gauntlet of formidable cypresses to reach the fortified hilltop town of Volpaia. To look at the tiny piazza—little more than a café, a stone well, and a rustic campanile—it seems a sleepy oasis in this tourist-mobbed region. But behind the crumbling walls, there's something surprising going on, for through Volpaia's ancient stone heart pumps 100 percent *vino*. Under your very feet, beneath a thin skin of pavement, arteries of tubular steel are secretly carrying the life's blood of the Chianti from

A Winery in Disguise

CASTELLO DI VOLPAIA, NEAR RADDA IN CHIANTI

chamber to chamber on its journey to winehood. Walking the little warren of streets, you'd never guess that behind a set of massive 15th-century doors yeasty grape juice bubbles away in huge stainless-steel tanks in a gleaming white tile room; that within a Renaissance church's crypt musty oaken casks add time and woody richness to the blend; or that from the rafters of a 600-year-old attic grapes hang to dry and sweeten before their transformation into *vin santo*, the traditional dessert wine. A guided tour comes with your room key when you stay in one of the antique houses that, along with the vineyard and most of the town, were a father's wedding gift to his daughter three decades ago. Stock up on whatever your nose fancies at the *enoteca*, then retire to your private rose garden overlooking the sun-warmed fields to savor the fruit of the vine, which here is truly the point of it all.

Sangiovese grapes give Chianti Classico, like Volpaia's esteemed version, its distinctive ruby red color, spicy fragrance, and touch of fruitiness.

All the Details

Prices reflect the full range in a category throughout the year and are given in dollars only when the supplier quotes in dollars (exchange rate at press time: 1,672 lire to the U.S. dollar). Properties are open **year-round** and accept **credit cards**, and rooms have **private baths**, unless otherwise stated. When writing, remember to add "Italy" to the **address**; when **phoning or faxing**, dial 011-39, then the number, including the initial zero. Since there's often no one who **speaks English** in places off the beaten track, written requests for information or a reservation work best, phrased as simply as possible and faxed; the many Web sites given here should help. **APT** is the short form for Azienda di Promozione Turistica, or tourist office.

CASENTINO

The sparsely populated Casentino–immortalized by Dante as the source of the Arno, high on Monte Falterona, and the site of the final battle of the Guelph-Ghibelline war, in which he fought–has enough castles, little Romanesque churches, and unspoiled villages to keep you happily exploring for days. But the jewels in its crown, contained within the 89,000-acre Casentino Forests National Park, straddling Tuscany and Emilia-Romagna, are La Verna and Camaldoli monasteries. The twisting 21-mile mountain road between the two makes a stunning drive in spring, when every bend brings another stirring vista: forested slopes in every shade of green cut with deep slashes of dark silver firs, crags of bare rock, pillowy-soft emerald fields, white cattle grazing by the roadside, and fountains of yellow broom. In fall, elm, maple, beech, and ash trees wreath parts of the mountains in a bright coronal of red and gold.

LA VERNA AND CAMALDOLI MONASTERIES (9D-E)

A Forest of Mysteries, p.46

The Casentino Forests National Park is threaded through with sparkling streams and rushing waterfalls that tumble down to the valley—and with well-marked walking trails that take you to them. Two miles below the hermitage—where Romualdo's original cell, model for the other cottages, is outside the gate and open to visitors—is Camaldoli's monastery, with a church (frescoes by Spinello Aretino,

EMILIA-ROMAGNA
Imola
Faenza
Parco dell' Orecchiella
GARFAGNANA
Gramolazzo
Camporgiano
San Pellegrino in Alpe
Carrara
Rif. Donegani
Lago di Vagli
Rif. Nello Conti
Castelnuovo
Resceto
Monte Altissimo
Barga
Massa
Natural Park of the Apuan Alps
Grotta del Vento
Seravezza
Bagni di Lucca
Pietrasanta
MUGELLO
Sieve
Pistoia
Villa Mansi
Villa Torrigiani
Villa Reale
Viareggio
Prato
Lucca
Monte Falterona
Casentino Forests National Park
Capo d'Arno
Torre del Lago
Lago di Massaciuccoli
Fiesole
Eremo di Camaldoli
Stia
Camaldoli
Badia Prataglia
S. Rossore Natural Reserve
Firenze
Fattoria Il Milione
Pisa
Arno
Poppi
La Verna
CASENTINO
PRATOMAGNO
San Miniato
Bibbiena
Greve
Uzzano
Greve
Livorno
Elsa
Pesa
VIA CASSIA
Volpaia
Badia a Coltibuono
Radda
Poggio Alloro
Poggibonsi
Gaiole
Castellina
CHIANTI
Arezzo
San Gimignano
Castello di Brolio
Volterra
Siena
Arbia
Cécina
Cécina
Rapolano Terme
Ligurian Sca
CRETE
Sinalunga
COLLINE METALLIFERE
Amorosa
Ombrone
Monte Oliveto Maggiore
Buonconvento
Sant'Anna in Camprena

Ligurian Sea
Tyrrhenian Sea
Elba
Pianosa
Montecristo
Giglio
Giglio Castello
Pardini's Hermitage
Giannutri
Piombino
Cécina
Volterra
San Gimignano
Poggibonsi
Siena
Castello di Brolio
Rapolano Terme
Sinalunga
Amorosa
Sant'Anna in Camprena
Montepulc
Pienza
Monte Oliveto Maggiore
Buonconvento
Montalcino
Bagno Vignoni
S. Quírico d'Órcia
Ripa d'Órcia
La Torre
Monte Amiata
Radicófani
Massa Maríttima
COLLINE METALLIFERE
Grosseto
Spergolaia
Alberese
Regional Park of the Maremma
Talamone
Scansano
Saturnia
Sovana
Sorano
Pitigliano
Porto Santo Stefano
Monte Argentario
Porto Ercole
MAREMMA
LAZIO
Arno
Pesa
Elsa
Cécina
Ombrone
Orcia
Arbia
VIA CASSIA
Arez

paintings by Vasari) and a medieval pharmacy that sells the monks' liqueurs, teas, soaps, etc. La Verna's guest facilities are largely new and well-organized, with a public restaurant and simple rooms, including singles with private baths. St. Catherine of Siena received the second stigmata; more than 330 have been recorded to date.

DISTANCES: 50 mi from Florence, 70 mi from Siena, 165 mi from Rome.

FACILITIES: 100 beds in single, double, or larger rooms, with private or shared bath. Restaurant, shop.

PRICES: single 40,000 lire, double 50,000 lire, with private bath; 7,000 lire less with shared bath.

OPTIONS: A less austere base for exploring the Casentino is **Fattoria di Celli,** with 10 cozy, fireplaced apts. and 3 separate farmhouses on a tranquil hillside outside Poppi, views of the forested mountains, a sculpture garden, a tennis court, a playground and plenty of room for children to roam, and 2 beautifully landscaped pools on a wide lawn. 52013 Poppi (AR), tel. 0335/6056104 or 0575/529917, e-mail: celli@elledi.it or sbuijsen@wxs.nl; apts. 800,000–1,200,000 lire/wk for 2, 1,300,000–1,600,000 for 4, villa (for 4) 1,500,000–1,900,000 (daily rates possible Sept.–June). **Camaldoli** also has accommodation for guests, but it's more difficult to arrange in advance—it's simplest just to stop by and ask. Foresteria Monastero, 52010 Camaldoli (AR), tel. 0575/556013, e-mail: camaldoli@camaldoli.com, www.camaldoli.com.

CASENTINO HIGHLIGHTS

Castello dei Conti Guidi, an impressive 13th-century castle with moat and drawbridge, mullioned windows, frescoes, and a crenellated tower that dominates the entire area from its hilltop position in the walled town of **Poppi** (9E). **Badia Prataglia** (9D) abbey and crypt, built in 989 in pure Romanesque style. **Stia** (8D), with its appealing medieval Piazza Tanucci, lined with porticoed houses and a 12th-century Romanesque church boasting an Andrea della Robbia Madonna. **Church of San Francesco** in **Arezzo** (9F), with its great Piero della Francesco fresco cycle *Legend of the True Cross*. ALSO: **LA VERNA** (9E) and **CAMALDOLI** (9D) (*see* above).

CHIANTI

To many outsiders, Chianti *is* Tuscany. A region of hills whose every inch is covered with grapevines and olive trees held within dry stone terraces, it is achingly lovely, a perfectly civilized place of fortified towns, castles, and so many old farmhouses bought up and restored by the sun-seeking British that it has earned the nickname Chiantishire. Wine, grown here for 23 centuries, is Chianti's raison d'être, and along the endlessly twisting SS222, known as the Chiantigiana, signs point to hundreds of wineries offering tastings and tours. Those marked with the Gallo Nero, or Black Rooster—symbol of the Chianti League, a military association formed in the 14th century by the towns of Castellina, Gaiole, and Radda—are members of the Chianti Classico consortium, meaning they fall into the right geographic zone (between Florence and Siena) and abide by strict standards, including the "iron rule" for varietal proportions established by Baron Bettino Ricasoli in 1874. Recent vintages are celebrated in a mid-September wine festival in Greve in Chianti.

CASTELLO DI VOLPAIA, NEAR RADDA IN CHIANTI (7F)

A Winery in Disguise, p.78

Volpaia emerged around the 10th century, part of a chain of fortresses in this border area between Florentine and Sienese territories. In addition to wine, Volpaia today produces olive oil, aromatic vinegars, and chestnut, heather, and other honeys from hives placed throughout the thousand-acre estate. The apartments, in a 16th-century house or above the *frantoio,* are nicely furnished with antiques and prints. The cottages are spacious and private, with attractive pools, gardens, and views and lots of room for cooking and entertaining.

CONTACT: Apts.: Castello di Volpaia Agriturismo, Loc. Volpaia, 53017 Radda in Chianti (SI), tel. 0577/738066, fax 0577/738619, e-mail: volpaia@chianticlassico.com or info@volpaia.com, www.chianticlassico.com. Cottages: Villas International Ltd., 950 Northgate Dr. #206, San Rafael, CA 94903, tel. 800/221-2260 or 415/499-9490, fax 415/499-9491, e-mail: villas@best.com, www.villasintl.com.

DISTANCES: 25 mi from Florence, 24 mi from Siena, 130 mi from Rome.

FACILITIES: 5 apts. (1–3 bedrooms; 4 apts. can be combined) with TV and VCR, 3 with private garden, all share pool; 2 cottages (Casetto sleeps 8, La Pozza 11), each with private pool and garden. Cottages and some apts. have fireplaces. Tennis court (fee).

PRICES: Apts.: 800,000–1,750,000 lire/wk. Cottages: Casetto $2,760–$5,117 for 1 wk, $4,800–$8,900 for 2 wks; La Pozza $3,392–$6,440 for 1 wk, $5,900–$11,200 for 2 wks.

OPTIONS: To stay in Volpaia for less than a week, try one of the 2 clean, simple apartments (sleeping 2 or 4) in **Casa Selvolini,** owned by the same family for 300 years. La Volpaia, Radda in Chianti (SI), tel. 0577/738626, fax 0577/738329; 100,000 lire for 2. New in spring 1999, in a very secluded spot down a private road on the crest of a hill, is the **Locanda di Volpaia,** a just-built inn offering a spectacular view of Volpaia and its vine- and cypress-covered fields; 6 doubles and 1 suite with TV, cotto floors, and country furnishings (most with private

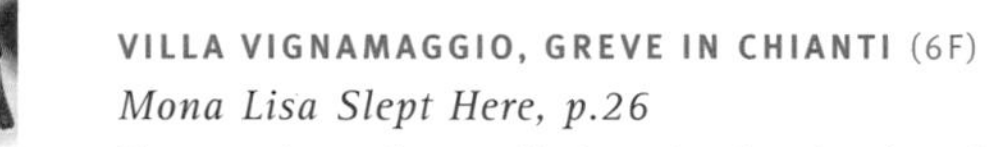

terrace); and a fireplaced salon, a small bar, a pool, light lunch, and dinner. 53017 Radda in Chianti (SI), tel./fax 0577/738833, e-mail: info@locandavolpaia.com; 250,000–350,000 lire with tax and breakfast; closed Christmas–Easter.

THE VILLA TABLE, BADIA A COLTIBUONO, GAIOLE IN CHIANTI (7F)

Cooking with Class, p.70

With a down-to-earth approach and (usually) a lot of patience and humor after hearing the same questions for 15 years, Milan-born Lorenza teaches a variety of regional styles in a big country kitchen with a marble-topped island where many hands can join in. Mostly American, guests are a varied mix—one session included a private chef, a nurse and her Italian-born mother, the CFO of an international conglomerate. The appealing guest rooms are in the 11th- and 16th-century parts of the former Benedictine abbey, in Lorenza's husband's family since 1846. The garden is a dreamy place, with roses and herbs, a pergola for shaded walks, box hedges, koi pools, and tinkling fountain. Dinners out are a rare opportunity to experience extraordinary Tuscan homes and hospitality—possibly worth the price alone.

CONTACT: The Villa Table, Badia a Coltibuono, 53013 Gaiole in Chianti (SI), tel. 0577/749498, fax 0577/749235, e-mail: coltibuono@chianticlassico.com, www.chianticlassico.com/coltibuono. Or Judy Ebrey, P.O. Box 25228, Dallas, TX 75225, tel. 214/373–1161, fax 214/373–1162, e-mail: cuisineint@aol.com.

DISTANCES: 30 mi from Florence, 15 mi from Siena, 140 mi from Rome.

DATES (1999): May 10–15, June 7–12, June 21–26, June 30–July 5 (Palio week), Sept. 6–11, Sept. 27–Oct. 2, Oct. 4–9, Oct. 18–23.

FACILITIES: 8 doubles, 1 single. Library, concierge service, outdoor pool, garden, Tuscan restaurant, shop.

PRICES: Including five nights' lodgings, four days of classes, all meals and excursions: double, $3,500/person; single, $4,100. Palio week supplement (including prime seats at the starting line): $490/person.

OPTIONS: Giuliano Bugialli, another noted cookbook author and PBS cooking series star, has run a very hands-on cooking school since 1973. Guests are lodged at a Florence hotel and bused daily to his centuries-old farmhouse for classes, excursions, and dinners out. Giuliano Bugialli's Cooking in Florence, 60 Sutton Place S, #1KS, New York, NY 10022, tel. 212/813–9552, fax 212/486–5518; $3,600/wk all-inclusive, 6 courses May–Dec.

VILLA VIGNAMAGGIO, GREVE IN CHIANTI (6F)

Mona Lisa Slept Here, p.26

Vignamaggio, 2 miles outside Greve, is a luxurious base for touring Chianti. Rooms in the main house are airy and elegantly appointed: casement windows with leafy views, puffy feather comforters, light cooking facilities built into armoires, dining tables, sofas, antiques, prints. Others are in homey scattered stone farmhouses, each with a common room where breakfast is served, and there is a private cottage in the woods with a cheerful stone patio. Cooking and painting courses and dinners with wine tastings are available.

CONTACT: Villa Vignamaggio, Via Petriolo 5, 50022 Greve in Chianti (FI), tel. 055/854661, fax 055/8544468, e-mail: vignamaggio@pn.itnet.it, www.vignamaggio.com.

DISTANCES: 15 mi from Florence, 20 mi from Siena, 155 mi from Rome

FACILITIES: 1 room, 1 suite, 1 apt. in main house, 13 apts. (sleep 2–4) in farmhouses, 1 cottage, all with phone and light cooking facilities, some with Jacuzzi. Restaurant (guests only, two nights a week), 2 pools, (tired) tennis court, garden.

PRICES: double 230,000 lire, suite 270,000 lire, apt. 290,000–420,000 lire.

OPTIONS: Nonguests can see Vignamaggio's gardens and brick-vaulted wine cellars and have a **wine tasting** with advance reservations. Elsewhere in Chianti, **Relais Fattoria Vignale** is an elegant country hotel with frescoed salons, a stunning breakfast patio overlooking the pool and vineyards, a noted restaurant, and full amenities. Via Pianigiani 9, 53017 Radda in Chianti (SI), tel. 0577/738300, fax 0577/738592, e-mail: vignale@chiantinet.it; single 200,000–210,000 lire, double 260,000–360,000 lire, including breakfast buffet.

CHIANTI HIGHLIGHTS

Castello di Brolio (7G), since 1141 the family castle of the Ricasoli family, with mighty bastions, towers, and spectacular views of Siena, the surrounding vineyards, and the Arbia river valley; at the winery, one of Chianti's most important, the cellars may be visited and tastings arranged. Flower-filled **Vertine,** near **Gaiole in Chianti** (7F), and **Montefioralle,** outside **Greve in Chianti** (6F), two tiny medieval castle-hamlets that remain almost intact. **Castellina in Chianti's Via delle Volte** (6F), a 15th-century covered passageway for soldiers within the town walls, complete with vaulted roof and narrow arrow slits. The 18th-century Italian-style garden of the winemaking estate **Castello di Uzzano** (7E), with fountains, sculptures, reflecting pools, a maze, box hedges, climbing roses, and huge old ornamental trees (sequoia, cedars of Lebanon and the Himalayas); the wine shop will sell you a picnic to eat on the formal terrace under a romantic white canopy.

CRETE SENESI AND THE VAL D'ÓRCIA

Head south from Siena, past the vine-stitched hills of Chianti, into a landscape of more variety and wider vistas. This is postcard country, where a lone cypress or farmhouse on a rise amid a field of grain levitates cameras out of their cases, where limestone cliffs jut up unexpectedly as you round a bend in the road, and where eerie stretches of barren clay hills *(crete)* gave even the gothic Hawthorne and de Sade the willies. Though the real pleasure of a visit is in the journey more than the destinations, that is not to say that there aren't any. Tool up to hilltop fortresses like Radicofani and Rocca d'Órcia, in the Val d'Órcia; walk the streets of Pienza, bursting at its flower-edged seams with shops selling the local pecorino, wild boar, and mushrooms; and build your calf muscles exploring the medieval hilltowns of Montepulciano and Montalcino and your biceps carrying away their famous wines—ending at one of the many spas in this thermal hotbed to soothe whatever aches you've created.

AGRITURISMO LA TORRE, NEAR PIENZA (8I)

The Art of the Landscape, p.32

About 9 miles from Pienza, La Torre has two pleasant apartments. The smaller one, downstairs, is one room with a barrel-vaulted ceiling, a kitchenette, a Murphy bed, stuffed armchairs, a dining table, and a window looking out to the patio. The larger, on three floors, has a dining room/kitchenette/living room with sofabed and woodburning fireplace and, upstairs, a big bedroom with a beam-and-brick ceiling, nice views, and the pretty antique bed; a curtain shields the room from the stairway to a second, similar bedroom under sloping eaves.

CONTACT: Agriturismo La Torre, Loc. La Vittoria, 53026 Pienza (SI), tel./fax 0578/755037. Useful regional Web site: www.nautilus-mp.com/tuscany

DISTANCES: 85 mi from Florence, 42 mi from Siena, 100 mi from Rome.

FACILITIES: 2 apts. (1 bedroom/1 bath, 2 bedrooms/2 baths) with kitchenette. Use of pool at sister property near Chianciano, the spa town.

PRICES: 550,000 lire/wk for small apt. (sleeps 2), 900,000–1,100,000 lire/wk for large one (sleeps 4 or 5), in summer; call for other rates.

OPTIONS: If the idea of biking through the fields and hilltowns of the Crete (or elsewhere in Tuscany) appeals, hop on one of **Bike Riders Tours'** routes, including one with a Tuscan chef biking alongside you, escorting you to his favorite wine cellars and markets, and giving a hands-on lesson; there's also a self-guided tour. Box 130254, Boston, MA 02113, tel. 800/473-7040 or 617/723-2354, fax 617/723-2355; 6 or 7 nights, $1,760–$2,780/person. For a stone tower in the **Maremma,** *see* WHERE SKY MELTS INTO SEA. For one at the edge of a Chianti vineyard and olive grove a 20-minute walk from Radda, there's the 2-bedroom **Torre di Canvalle,** with beamed ceilings, stone walls, a fireplace, a circular staircase, simple antiques, and a shared pool. 53017 Radda in Chianti (SI), tel. 0577/738321; $650/wk. Or Italy Farm Holidays, 547 Martling Ave., Tarrytown, NY 10591, tel. 914/631-7880, fax 914/631-8831, e-mail: italyfarms@aol.com; $950/wk.

BALLOONING IN TUSCANY, RAPOLANO TERME (8G)

Up, Up, and Away, p.76

Ballooning depends on the weather—if the conditions aren't right, you don't fly (there's a 15% cancellation rate), and if the winds act up during a flight, there may be some bumps on landing. The winds also determine your direction, so there's no telling where you'll end up or what you'll see—only that it'll be great. Flights last 60 to 90 minutes, after about 40 minutes helping the pilot, Englishman Robert Etherington, who's lived in Tuscany for a decade, to get the balloon inflated and ready to go. The Rapolano B&B, run by young mother Giorgia Kirchner, offers simple, nicely decorated rooms in a farmhouse with a pretty garden and fine views over the rolling hills of the Crete.

CONTACT: Ballooning in Tuscany, Via dei Goti 17, 53040 Rapolano Terme (SI), tel. 0577/725517, fax 0577/725519, e-mail: etherington@ftbcc.it, www.ballooningintuscany.com. B&B: Podere Il Fornacino, 53040 Rapolano Terme (SI), tel. 0577/725509 (the owner speaks little English, but Ballooning in Tuscany can make reservations for you, here or elsewhere, and many other kinds of touring arrangements).

DISTANCES: 50 mi from Florence, 10 mi from Siena, 140 mi from Rome.

FACILITIES: B&B: 2 doubles with bath, 2 doubles share one large bath.

PRICES: Flight: 1 hour with glass of champagne, 250,000 lire/person for up to 4 people; 1.5 hours with champagne breakfast for 2, 350,000 lire/person. Flights May–Oct. B&B: double 50,000 lire/person.

OPTIONS: For 100,000 lire more, you can take off from **Locanda dell'Amorosa** (*see* LOVE IN BLOOM) or other locations. **The Very Private Europe of Buddy Bombard** offers a weeklong luxury ballooning experience, including midair feasts, lunches with Tuscan nobility, escorted tours, and prime seats for Siena's Palio (*see* Options in RAW SIENA). **Maremma Mongolfiera** flies from the Saturnia area and is connected with an agritourism farm. Loc. Pianetti, 58050 Montemerano (GR), tel. 0564/602627, e-mail: piancasali@laltramaremma.it, www.laltramaremma.it; flights 250,000 lire/person. Another way to get an overview of Tuscany is by chartered small plane or helicopter with **Delta Aerotaxi.** Florence Airport, 50100 Firenze, tel. 055/315250,

fax 055/318491, e-mail: delta.aerotaxi@flashnet.it. To see the Crete from a bit closer to the ground ride the **Nature Train,** a tourist line of the Val d'Órcia Railway that travels between Asciano and Monte Antico along rivers and streams, panoramic ridges and viaducts, on holidays spring through fall. APT, Il Campo 56, 53100 Siena, tel. 0577/280551, fax 0577/270676.

LOCANDA DELL'AMOROSA, NEAR SINALUNGA (8H)

Love in Bloom, p.40

Most of Amorosa's accommodations live up to the beauty of the setting and the height of the prices; even the unrenovated, marbleless-bathrooms often compensate with quirky charms, like the great view from the clock tower room's tub. Each has its own character, so ask for details when booking, but in general they are charming and comfortable, with preserved period details (like suite #44's huge peasant fireplace with a seat in it), antique furnishings and prints, and restful views over the garden, fields, or piazza. A new apartment in an old farm building set off by itself is set to open in 1999 and should be lovely, with a fireplaced sitting room, a rose garden, and a view of the sun setting over the vineyards.

CONTACT: Locanda dell'Amorosa, Loc. Amorosa, 53048 Sinalunga (SI), tel. 0577/679497, fax 0577/632001, e-mail: locanda.amorosa@inter-business.it.

DISTANCES: 53 mi from Florence, 26 mi from Siena, 105 mi from Rome.

FACILITIES: 9 rooms, 8 1- and 2-bedroom suites, 1 new 1-bedroom apt. with kitchen, all with private bath, minibar, direct-dial phone, TV, air-conditioning, safe; some fireplaces. Restaurant, wine bar/restaurant, shop selling wine and local produce. Wine and olive oil tastings and cooking classes by arrangement.

PRICES: double 360,000–420,000 lire, suite 490,000–550,000 lire, including breakfast buffet, tax, and service. Closed Jan.–Feb.

MILLE MIGLIA CLASSIC-CAR ROAD RALLY, VIA CASSIA (9K-6D)

The Great Road Show, p.58

The original Mille Miglia covered the "Thousand Miles" of its title non-stop, with a record time of 10 hours—incredible speed considering the largely unpaved roads of the day and the many little villages passed through. First run in 1927, it was stopped for the second and final time in 1957 after a crash that left 12 people dead. Today's three-day re-creation has been altered to balance safety with a reasonable amount of thrill. A reflection of Italians' love of driving and the crazy risk-taking that is obvious on any Italian road any day, it draws crowds all along the route, from cars pulled over at strategic points on the Via Cassia—built in the 2nd century B.C. to connect Rome with Florence—to urbanites convened in well-placed cafés to farm families gathered at card tables set up in their fields. At the Affittacamere L'Órcia, a guesthouse with clean, simple rooms in the ancient walled town of San Quírico d'Órcia (8I), you can sit on your own windowsill and wave like a privileged local as the cars pass slowly by on the narrow street below you, just a few feet from the checkpoint.

CONTACT: Race info: Comitato Organizzatore Mille Miglia, Via Cassala 60, 25126 Brescia (LO), tel. 030/280036, fax 030/48093, www.1000-miglia.it. Affittacamere L'Órcia, Via Dante Alighieri 49, San Quírico d'Órcia (SI), tel. 0577/897677 (no fax, no English, but they manage).

FACILITIES: 12 rooms. Sunny terrace, bar downstairs.

PRICES: double 70,000 lire.

OPTIONS: You can stay anywhere near the route, including Florence, Siena, Monte Oliveto Maggiore, Sant'Anna in Camprena, Pienza, and Ripa d'Órcia, all covered elsewhere in this book. A mile or so outside Pienza and right off the Via Cassia, with a sweeping view of the race, is **Agriturismo La Fonte,** offering 4 apts. in a 15th-century stone farmhouse, a lighted pool, and a playground, set amid the fields and soft clay hills of the Crete. Podere Fonte Bertusi di Sopra 73, 53026 Pienza (SI), tel./fax 0578/749142 or tel. 0578/748470, cell 0368/3751643; 100,000–140,000 lire/day for 2; no credit cards.

MONTE OLIVETO MAGGIORE (7H)

Stairway to Heaven, p.54

Monte Oliveto is the most visited monastery in Tuscany; it even has a tourist office covering the Crete Senesi. Sundays draw the biggest crowds, so to avoid sharing the frescoes with busloads of schoolchildren, plan a weekday visit. The very simple, unheated *foresteria* (guesthouse), converted from the ancient stables, can accommodate individuals or families; males seeking a spiritual retreat of a week or longer can request a stay with the monks in the monastery itself. Sung chants are featured at the 11 a.m. Mass on Sunday and at a special midnight Mass on Christmas Eve.

CONTACT: Monte Oliveto Maggiore, 53020 Chiusure (SI), tel. 0577/707061.

DISTANCES: 62 mi from Florence, 22 mi from Siena, 131 mi from Rome.

FACILITIES: 30 rooms (sleep 2–4) with shared baths. Restaurant, shop.

PRICES: 30,000 lire/person. Foresteria closed Nov.–Mar.

OPTIONS: For a monastery experience more removed from the world, *see* A FOREST OF MYSTERIES.

RIPA D'ÓRCIA, VAL D'ÓRCIA (8I)

Keys to the Castle, p.8

Ripa d'Órcia is light on amenities, and simply appointed, but comfortable—best are the apartments with terrace and fireplace. The restaurant, presided over by family members, serves good Tuscan home cooking and the estate's wines. The walk to Bagno Vignoni (seen in Tarkovsky's film *Nostalghia*) is one of many in *Walking and Eating in Tuscany and Umbria,* a terrific book by James Lasdun and Pia Davis. Swimming in the piazza is no longer allowed, but the thermal pool at the Hotel Posta Marcucci is a wonder, with a bar and great view.

CONTACT: Ripa d'Órcia, 53023 Castiglione d'Órcia (SI), tel. 0577/897376 or 0577/897317, fax 0577/898038, e-mail: ripa.dorcia@comune.siena.it, www.nautilus-mp.com/ripa. Hotel Posta Marcucci: tel. 0577/887112.

DISTANCES: 74 mi from Florence, 28 mi from Siena, 124 mi from Rome.

FACILITIES: 6 doubles, 7 apts. (5 with fireplace, 5 with terrace) sleeping 2–4. Restaurant (dinner Tues.–Sun.), common room with piano.

PRICES: double 150,000–170,000 lire, including breakfast, tax, and service; apt. 850,000 lire/wk for 2, 1,250,000 lire for 4, including tax. Rooms closed Nov., Jan. 7–Feb.; apts. closed Nov.–Mar. Posta Marcucci pool: 18,000 lire, shower and towel 6,000 lire; closed Nov.–May.

OPTIONS: For a luxury version of a castle, the 11th-century **Castello di Spaltenna** is a country hotel with 26 rooms and suites with TVs, some canopy beds; views of Chianti's hills, woods, and vineyards; gardens and a landscaped pool with a waterfall; an indoor pool with sauna; an old wine cellar bar with brick-vaulted ceiling; a fine restaurant with outdoor dining in the cloister; and a new tennis court. 53013 Gaiole in Chianti (SI), tel. 0577/749483, fax 0577/749269; double 310,000–395,000 lire, suites with fireplace 450,000–490,000 lire.

SANT'ANNA IN CAMPRENA, NEAR PIENZA (8H)

An Abandoned Monastery, p.22

Accommodations at Sant'Anna, a few miles outside Pienza (whose 15th-century piazza also appeared in the film), are spartan, though they're being upgraded slowly. The room with Sodoma's frescoes wasn't used in the film; since the church, which owns Sant'Anna, balked at allowing a wall to be knocked down for camera access, the room was re-created upstairs. Courses in Italian language and culture, taught in comfortable classrooms on the premises, are available. Rooms are often booked by U.S. and German college groups.

CONTACT: Azienda Agricola Sant'Anna in Camprena, 53026 Pienza (SI), tel. 0578/748303 (after 4 p.m.) or tel./fax 0578/748037, e-mail: serafinic@bccmp.com, www.nautilus-mp.com/tuscany/aziende/sanna.

DISTANCES: 90 mi from Florence, 30 mi from Siena, 90 mi from Rome.

FACILITIES: 4 doubles with bath; 30 rooms (sleep 1–4) with shared bath, closed Nov.–Mar.; 3 newly renovated apts. out back. Dining room, shop selling farm products.

PRICES: double (approximately; all is negotiable) 50,000 lire/person with breakfast, apt. 80,000–150,000 lire for 2–4. Courses: 30-hour week, 1,000,000 lire; 40,000 lire per hour.

CRETE SENESI HIGHLIGHTS

Pienza (8I), rebuilt by Pope Pius II to make his hometown a model of Renaissance urban planning, with a superbly harmonious cathedral piazza, a walkable city wall with a great valley view, tidy back streets spilling with flowerpots and windowboxes, plus museums, good cafés, and lots of shops selling local foods; Zeffirelli's *Romeo and Juliet* was filmed here. The winemaking hilltowns of **Montalcino** (7I), famous for its Brunello, perhaps Tuscany's most respected wine, and **Montepulciano** (9H), known for its Vino Nobile, Brunello's competition; both with warrens of intact medieval streets, plenty of wine shops, wine cellars, and everything wine. ALSO: **BAGNO VIGNONI** (8I) and the frescoed cloister of **MONTE OLIVETO MAGGIORE** (7H) (*see* above).

FLORENCE

If ever a city could be called a treasure house of art, it is Florence. Throughout the Renaissance, which was invented here, the streets ran with great artists, who left their work behind them in every piazza, fortresslike *palazzo,* and marble-frosted church—and in one of the world's great museums, the Uffizi. But Florence is also a vibrant city with half a million inhabitants, schools full of foreign art and language students, and excellent restaurants and shopping. It's a great walking city, with tiny alleys and broad, café-rimmed piazzas and covered markets. A river runs through it, softening the sometimes forbidding architecture. And at the edge of it all is the green oasis of the Boboli Gardens, with its fountains, grottoes, and winding paths. Don't visit in summer if you can help it—it's deadly hot, horribly crowded, and packed with traffic. Spring and fall are ideal.

FATTORIA IL MILIONE DI BRANDIMARTE GUSCELLI, NEAR FLORENCE *(6E)*

Nectar of the Gods, p.14

Owner Jessica Husy's late husband, Brandimarte, a silversmith who created goblets and bowls crusted with daffodils, grapes, and other

motifs from nature, also created this farm as a work of art. Paths wind among lawns, olive trees, huge urns filled with flowers, sculptures, cozy nooks for reading, and a nicely landscaped pool. Dinners on the patio under a wisteria-covered pergola are Tuscan magic. Accommodations are in Jessica's house and in rebuilt farmhouses, some adjacent, three antiques-filled ones a half-mile away. Olives are picked for about two months, starting sometime in November.

CONTACT: Fattoria il Milione di Brandimarte Guscelli, Via di Giogoli 14, 50124 Firenze, tel. 055/2048713, fax 055/2048046.

DISTANCES: 4 mi from Florence, 37 mi from Siena, 170 mi from Rome.

FACILITIES: 7 apts. (2 sleep 2, 5 sleep 4) with full kitchens, heat, most with phone and TV, some with fireplace. Outdoor pool, garden, bocce court, playground, pond for fishing, 6 horses for experienced riders only (no guide), walking and jogging paths.

PRICES: 150,000 lire/night, 980,000 lire/wk, for 2 (double for 4). 3-night minimum year-round. Dinner: 50,000 lire. No credit cards.

OPTIONS: Castello di Volpaia (*see* A WINERY IN DISGUISE) will let you watch oil being pressed at its *frantoio* by previous arrangement.

FIREWORKS, FEAST OF SAN GIOVANNI (6D)

Baptism of Fire, p.64

The Feast of San Giovanni, on June 24, is celebrated all day, with processions of costumed trumpeters, drummers, and flagtossers, speeches in the Palazzo Vecchio, a concert in the Duomo, and a Mass in the Baptistery. Best of all is the Calcio in Costume, a wild soccer game played in medieval dress on a grandstand-ringed sand field created in the piazza of Santa Croce (advance tickets a must; ask at the tourist office). To watch from the Piazzale Michelangelo, a terrace with an incredible view of the city, walk there along paths that lead up the hillside. If you book the penthouse at the Continental, at the foot of the Ponte Vecchio, you can watch from your private balcony one floor above the roof terrace; the bedroom is set into a 12th-century tower—you'll wake to a view of the Palazzo Vecchio and the Duomo on one side, the river and the bridge on the other. Several other rooms, like #656, have perfect river views.

CONTACT: Hotel Continental, Lungarno Accaiuoli 2, 50123 Firenze, tel. 055/27262, fax 055/283139, e-mail: lungarnohotels@lungarnohotels.it, www.lungarnohotels.it.

FACILITIES: 45 rooms and suites, with marble baths, air conditioning, direct-dial phones with separate fax/modem line, satellite TV. Bar, lounges (with window walls looking directly onto the Ponte Vecchio), roof terrace, Internet credit card terminal, limo service, garaging.

PRICES: single 330,000 lire, double 400,000–450,000 lire, suite 580,000–760,000 lire, including tax, service, and breakfast.

OPTIONS: If you like your fireworks loud and close, at the **Hotel River,** on the water directly across from the Piazzale Michelangelo, you can watch in comfort with other guests from the 19th-century palazzo's stone balcony or from the window of your own front room (#27 has an antique coffered ceiling). Lungarno della Zecca Vecchia 18, 50122 Firenze, tel. 055/23443529, fax 055/2343531, e-mail: hotelriver@iol.it, www.hotelriver.it; double 220,000–260,000 lire with breakfast. When fireworks aren't involved, the Continental's Oltrarno sister property, **Hotel Lungarno,** is a wonderful option on the river, with private terraces—some amazingly spacious—facing the Duomo, the Badia, the Palazzo Vecchio, well, just about everything; new crisp white-and-navy decor by the very fashionable Italian family who own the hotels; and hundreds of artworks, including Picasso and Cocteau drawings. Borgo San Jacopo 14, 50125 Firenze, tel. 055/27261, fax 055/268437, e-mail: lungarnohotels@lungarnohotels.it, www.lungarnohotels.it; double 450,000–510,000 lire, including tax, service, and breakfast.

TORRE DI BELLOSGUARDO (6D)

A Pool with a View, p.56

All of Torre di Bellosguardo's accommodations have their charms, like a gilded four-poster bed, and views of either Florence, the back garden—pergolas draped in wisteria or climbing roses, a water garden with lily pond and cascading pools, plantings marked with their botanical names—or the rolling countryside, covered with olive groves and cypresses. The choicest, though, are the spacious corner rooms—#6 (the best, with coffered ceilings, a huge antique casement bed surrounded by a built-in step, and a living room with ornately carved walls and a decorative stone hearth fireplace), #9, and #12—which have the city view and good antiques. The tower suite, a vast, high-ceilinged space with a skylit sleeping loft reached by a narrow, suspended staircase, is really too sparely decorated but has fine views on all four sides and windowseats to watch them from. A new solarium in the greenhouse, lush with tropical plants, is a welcoming retreat in winter.

CONTACT: Torre di Bellosguardo, Via Roti Michelozzi 2, Firenze, tel. 055/2298145 or 055/2309046, fax 055/229008, e-mail: torredibellosguardo@dada.it.

DISTANCES: 40 mi from Siena, 170 mi from Rome.

FACILITIES: 8 doubles, 2 singles, 6 suites, all with direct-dial phones. Small bar, outdoor pool (mid-May–mid-Oct.) with poolside lunches and drinks, solarium; indoor pool planned for winter '99–'00.

PRICES: single 290,000–340,000 lire, double 450,000 lire, suites 550,000–650,000 lire, including tax.

FLORENCE HIGHLIGHTS

Besides the obvious, two beautifully restored, wonderful fresco cycles: the **Brancacci Chapel,** by Masaccio, Masolino, and Filippino Lippi, at Santa Maria del Carmine; and Gozzoli's *Journey of the Magi,* in the **Palazzo Medici-Riccardi,** full of rich colors, gilding, characterful portraiture of various Medici, and naturalistic detail. **Museo di San Marco,** 15th-century Dominican monastery where Fra Angelico lived, decorating each monk's cell with frescoes and a hallway with an ethereally lovely Annunciation; a room filled with his exquisitely colored and gilded paintings. Tombs at the **Cappella Medicee,** designed by Michelangelo. **Mercato Centrale,** a big, colorful covered food hall. **San Miniato al Monte,** an 11th-century Romanesque church on a hilltop, with a huge gilded apse mosaic by Ravenna artisans and a fantastic view of the city and river. **Fiesole** (6D), a leafy village on a hilltop with a panoramic view of Florence, ruins of an Etruscan temple and a Roman amphitheater and thermal baths, and several good museums.

GARFAGNANA AND LUCCA

Lucca is an utterly charming town you'll want to linger in. As medievally correct as the next guy, with its handful of memorable churches, museums, villas, and palaces (like Palazzo Pfanner, seen in Jane Campion's *Portrait of a Lady*), it is also bursting with life. Bicycles careen along the narrow streets or circle the town on a path through a tree-shaded park high atop a 2.5-mile ring of ramparts. After sampling Lucca's good shops and *trattorie,* head for the hills to explore villas built over the centuries by silk merchants, bankers, and other influential families. Or follow the river Serchio north to the Garfagnana–a rough, virtually untouristed green valley sandwiched between two mountain ranges–for something completely different. About 15 miles out of the city is Bagni di Lucca, a spa resort whose hot springs and scenery drew so many English visitors in the 18th and 19th centuries, including Byron and Shelley, that it has an English cemetery. More characteristic of the Garfagnana's rural character is the Orecchiella, a mountainous park of thick chestnut, fir, and beech woods, little ponds and streams, and alpine pasturelands dotted with stone shepherds' huts.

MULIN DEL RANCONE, CAMPORGIANO (2B)

By the Old Mill Stream, p.36

When you've tortured the kids enough with museums and churches, give them a break in a place where they can fish, swim, birdwatch, ride horses, and run around on acres of grass. The *mulino* also makes an inexpensive romantic getaway and a good base for exploring the Garfagnana or the marble quarries of the Apuan Alps (*see* INTO THE MARBLE MOUNTAINS). The local farms that jointly own the *mulino* provide most of the ingredients that end up on its tables. Rooms are very simple; the four in the mill are more atmospheric, with brick-and-beam ceilings, old hearths, a few sweet prints, and the view (you can see the fish swimming in the crystal clear water below your window).

CONTACT: Mulin del Rancone, Camporgiano (LU), tel./fax 0583/618670, e-mail: M.Rancone@mclink.it, www.garfprod.it.

DISTANCES: 75 mi from Florence, 105 mi from Siena, 250 mi from Rome.

FACILITIES: 8 doubles with phone; TV in common room. Restaurant, small bar, horseback riding with guide (10 horses; must reserve ahead), river swimming in summer, mountain-bike rental, sports field. There's also a camping area.

PRICES: 60,000 lire with breakfast, 85,000 lire half-board, 110,000 lire full board (all per person); closed Jan.–Feb.

THE VILLAS OF THE LUCCAN HILLS (3D)

La Dolce Vita, p.66

Villa Reale's gardens include elaborate *jeux d'eaux* and grottoes that drip water at the touch of a button. Inside Villa Torrigiani—whose gardens are attributed to the hand that landscaped Versailles, Le Nôtre—are palatial furnishings, Sèvres porcelain, frescoes, and works by important 17th- and 18th-century European artists. The architect who transformed Torrigiani's facade did the same for nearby Villa Mansi. The gardens—half English, half Italian—feature ponds, cascades, and statues; furnishings include canopy beds draped in 18th-century Luccan silks. The gardens of Villa Bernardini, lived in by the same family who built it in the early 17th century, include a trilevel green theater where concerts for up to 600 guests are sometimes held. Rentable are Villa Mansi Bernardini and Villa Donati (shown, from left, in photos bottom p.68). Mansi Bernardini, an 18th-century shooting lodge high on a hill with a lovely view of the valley, is furnished with antiques and oil paintings and is the scene of culture-and-cooking classes taught by the owner in spring and fall. Highlights of Donati, with its simple 16th-century lines, are the arched loggia off the living room for alfresco dining and a pool set in a cypress-edged lawn with magnificent views. A Web site with a driving tour and tons of information on dozens of villas is www.comune.lucca.it/en-index.htm.

Tours: Villa Bernardini: Vicopelago, 4 km from Lucca via A11, exit Lucca, then 3 km; tel./fax 0583/370327; house and gardens. **Villa Mansi:** Segromigno in Monte, 12 km from Lucca via SS12 north; tel. 0583/920234, fax 0583/928114; house and gardens; closed Mon.

Villa Reale: Marlia, 8 km from Lucca via A11, exit Capannori; tel. 0583/30108, tel./fax 0583/30108 or 0583/30009; gardens open for guided tours only, at specific hours; closed Mon., and by appointment only Dec.–Feb. **Villa Torrigiani:** Camigliano, 10 km from Lucca via SS435 toward Pescia and Montecatini Terme, exit Capannori, 6 km; tel. 0583/928008, fax 0583/928041; house and gardens; closed Tues. and mid-Nov.–Feb.

Accommodations: Villa Donati (in Sant'Alessio), **Villa Mansi Bernardini** (in Segromigno), and others can be booked through Villas International Ltd., 950 Northgate Dr. #206, San Rafael, CA 94903, tel. 800/221-2260 or 415/499-9490, fax 415/499-9491, e-mail: villas@best.com, www.villasintl.com.

DISTANCES: 45 mi from Florence, 60 mi from Siena, 220 mi from Rome.

FACILITIES: Villa Donati: 1 double with dressing room and bath, 2 doubles with bath, 2 doubles and 1 single room share a bath. Fireplaced sitting and dining rooms, pool, garden. **Villa Mansi Bernardini:** 2 doubles with bath, 2 doubles share a bath. Pool, garden, tennis court.

PRICES: Villa Donati: 1 wk $7,235, 2 wks $12,460, including 18 hours/wk maid service. **Villa Mansi-Bernardini:** 1 wk $8,045, 2 wks $13,670, including 58 hours/wk maid and ironing services.

OPTIONS: Locanda l'Élisa, once the home of an official in the *principessa*'s retinue, is the loveliest of the villa hotels, with 10 small but sumptuous bedrooms (one with a little private yard) and several grand salons, all decorated in 18th-century French style; a pool gorgeously landscaped with a bridge and masses of flowers; and a restaurant in a Victorian conservatory. Via Nuova/Pisa, 55050 Massa Pisana (LU), tel. 0583/379737, fax 0583/379019, e-mail: locanda.elisa@lunet.it, www.relaischateaux.fr/elisa; double 420,000–480,000 lire, jr. suite 450,000–590,000 lire. An inexpensive option with homey charm is **Villa Casanova,** converted from a *fattoria,* with 40 simple rooms in three buildings, an outdoor pool, a tennis court, stables nearby, and farmland, woods, and excellent biking terrain all around. 55050 Balbano (LU), tel. 0583/548429, fax 0583/368955; double 110,000 lire.

GARFAGNANA AND LUCCA HIGHLIGHTS

Lucca's park on the bastions (*see* above); its **Guinigi Tower,** with oaks growing out of the roof and a panoramic view; its Pisan-Luccan Romanesque **Duomo,** with multicolor-marble façade; and its **Piazza Amfiteatro,** a beautiful, elliptical plaza following the layout of the Roman amphitheater formerly on the site and ringed with 19th-century buildings with flowers dripping from windowboxes. **Barga** (3C), a walled hilltown with narrow medieval streets that steeply climb to the cathedral for a spectacular valley view and some fine art pieces. **Lago di Vagli** (2B), a little crystal blue lake in a valley ringed by forested mountains. The **Museum of Country Life** in **San Pellegrino in Alpe** (3B), with 14 reconstructed rooms displaying more than 3,000 farm tools and household goods (spinning wheels, etc.) that demonstrate what life used to be like for the shepherds and peasants of this rural region.

MAREMMA

Over the past century, elaborate schemes involving a vast network of drainage canals have reclaimed the Maremma—a region virtually unknown to Americans—from malarial swampland into fertile farms where Italy's quickly disappearing cowboys can be seen herding a special breed of white cattle. Once a stronghold of the Etruscans, the area is rich with remains of this mysterious people, from monumental walls of towns built high on hills of tufa (volcanic rock) to tombs and other archeological sites that can be visited on drives through countryside that is impossibly green and velvety in spring. Along the Tyrrhenian Sea are popular beach resorts and a park encompassing seashore, pine forest, marsh, and *macchia* (scrubland). The best time to visit the park is September through May, when wildflowers are intense and birds fill the marshes; in the rainless summers, hours and trail access are very limited for fear of fire.

AZIENDA REGIONALE AGRICOLA DI ALBERESE (5K)

Riding with the Butteri, *p.60*

Riding alongside these cowboys is not for amateurs. It takes both stamina—you set off at 7 a.m. and cannot return until 11:30 or so—and the ability to control horses in varied terrains. A vast working farm within the Regional Park of the Maremma, the Azienda Regionale Agricola produces beef, grain, olive oil, wine, honey, and much more. The cattle, imported from Hungary and the steppes of Europe long ago and crossbred many times for hardiness, are raised to be yoked to farm equipment, and the meat of the young is sold at the farm. The branding of one-year-olds each May is another opportunity to watch the *butteri* at work. The apartments, in newly renovated farm buildings with lots of space around them (plus one in the villa), are simply furnished but comfortable and well-provisioned. The location is convenient for touring the park and the coast.

DISTANCES: 92 mi from Florence, 50 mi from Siena, 122 mi from Rome.

CONTACT: Azienda Regionale Agricola, Loc. Spergolaia, Alberese (GR), tel./fax 0564/407180 or 0564/407077. Parco Regionale della Maremma, Via del Fante, Alberese (GR), tel. 0564/407098, fax 0564/407278.

FACILITIES: 10 apts. sleeping 2–6, with fully equipped kitchens, TV; 1

2-bedroom apt. in villa with 2 baths, kitchen, living room, TV.

PRICES: July–Aug., 900,000 lire/wk for 2; Oct.–May, 600,000 lire/wk, 250,000 lire/wkend for 2. Ride with the *butteri:* 75,000 lire. No credit cards. Park admission is 7,000 lire, plus 2,000 lire for the bus to some trailheads; guides are available by reservation at 21,000 lire/hour.

LA TORCIATA DI SAN GIUSEPPE, PITIGLIANO (8K)

Rite of Spring, p.12

The Torciata takes place on March 19 and is preceded by a historical parade. Pitigliano was a haven for Jews fleeing the Papal States and developed a thriving community that's mostly gone now, though you'll still find the synagogue, a Jewish cemetery, and a Jewish bakery, and kosher wine continues to be produced. There's a palace, an art museum, and ancient churches to investigate, and ask about tours of the caves, later used as wine cellars, at the Civiltà Giubbonaia, a museum of objects unearthed in excavations of the tunnels they're displayed in. Albergo Guastini, the only hotel in town, has very basic rooms, but some have great views of the cliff it's perched on; the restaurant features Pitigliano's unique fusion Jewish-Tuscan cuisine.

CONTACT: Albergo Guastini, Piazza F. Petruccioli, 58017 Pitigliano (GR), tel. 0564/616065 or 0564/614106, fax 0564/616652, e-mail: htlguastini@laltramaremma.it, www.laltramaremma.it/alberghi/guastini. Tourist office: tel. 0564/617019, cell 0330/470198, fax 0564/617784. Web site on town: www.geocities.com/NapaValley/Vineyard/1399/pitigliano.html.

DISTANCES: 118 mi from Florence, 75 mi from Siena, 75 mi from Rome.

FACILITIES: 27 rooms with TV and phone. Restaurant.

PRICES: single 51,000 lire, double 85,000 lire, triple 115,000 lire. Closed Jan. 10—30.

PARDINI'S HERMITAGE, GIGLIO ISLAND (4M)

An Enchanted Isle, p.18

Aside from the inn's three little beaches, there are several public ones, served by bus from the port, or a boatman can drop you at private coves. The port has a few dive shops, and Campese beach, a café-lined crescent, has water sports facilities. At Arcobalena in Giglio Castello (also reachable by bus), a math teacher turned poet/restaurateur cooks up great fresh fish in former caves whimsically decorated with colorful local, Haitian, and other art. The little island of Giannutri (5M), about two hours away by ferry or private boat, is a good excursion with a ruin of a Roman villa. Wildflowers are best in April and May; the waters are swimmable mid-May to mid-October.

CONTACT: Pardini's Hermitage, Cala degli Alberi, 58013 Isola del Giglio (GR), tel. 0564/809034, fax 0564/809177, e-mail: hermit@ats.it, www.finalserv.it/hermitage. **Ferry reservations:** Toremar, tel. 0564/810803, fax 0564/818455, www.luda.livorno.it/toremar; 9,000 lire, car 40,400 lire. Maregiglio Navalgiglio, tel. 0564/812920, fax 0564/811056; 9,000 lire, car 45,000 lire; Apr.–Aug. only.

DISTANCES: To Porto Santo Stefano (1 hr from Giglio by ferry): 105 mi from Florence, 68 mi from Siena, 93 mi from Rome.

FACILITIES: 13 rooms and suites with phone; TV on request. Restaurant, 3 beaches, bocce, Ping-Pong, library, pottery workshop, musical instruments, bar.

PRICES: double 140,000–230,000 lire, suite 190,000–260,000 lire, full pension. 3-night minimum. Donkey rides: 120,000 lire/day. Boat trip: to/from port, 40,000 lire for up to 4 people; around island (2–3 hrs), 200,000 lire for 4. Packages built around pottery and watercolor classes are offered.

OPTIONS: **Affittacamere Angelo Landini** has 8 simple, clean apts. with cooking facilities and sea views in the piazza outside Giglio Castello. Giglio Castello, 58012 Isola del Giglio (GR), tel. 0564/806074; double 70,000–100,000 lire. Uphill a few steps is his brother's place, **Affittacamere Mario Landini,** with 6 sea-view rooms. Contrada S. Maria 12, Giglio Castello, 58012 Isola del Giglio (GR), tel. 0564/806076; double 70,000–100,000 lire. For accommodations within the medieval walls, contact agent **Piero Faccioli** at La Rocca, Via Roma 24, 58012 Isola del Giglio (GR), tel./fax 0564/806182.

TERME DI SATURNIA (7K)

Taking the Waters, p.48

In addition to pampering and exercise, Saturnia offers a doctor-staffed thermal-medicine institute with everything from hydromassage to treatments for periodontal, intestinal, even gynecological problems. The restaurant, with a window wall overlooking the pool, serves fine Mediterranean and Tuscan food, with buffets and a carving station ("dietetic program" available). Try to get to the Cascata before the crowds whose parked cars and RVs line the road each day. The steaming pools, less enjoyable in summer heat, are wonderful in winter, when you slip into them from the chilly or snowy air.

CONTACT: Terme di Saturnia, 58050 Saturnia (GR), tel. 0564/601061, fax 0564/601266, e-mail: info@termedisaturnia.it, www.termedisaturnia.it. Or Spa-Finders, 91 Fifth Ave., New York, NY 10003–3039, tel. 800/255–7727 or 212/924–6800, fax 212/924–7240.

DISTANCES: 124 mi from Florence, 80 mi from Siena, 104 mi from Rome.

FACILITIES: 80 rooms, 10 suites, with minibar, satellite and pay TV, VCR, IDD telephone, air conditioning. 4 outdoor thermal pools, sauna, steam bath, small gym, driving range, 2 lighted tennis courts, hair

salon, restaurant, poolside snack and cocktail bar and gelateria, boutique, piano bar, heliport; horseback riding at sister property.

PRICES: Vary by season, room class, meal plan, etc. Sample: With pools, sauna, Turkish bath, cosmetic consultation, all sports, breakfast, 225,000–445,000 lire/day, 1,085,000–3,115,000/wk, per person; cleansing facial, 90,000 lire.

OPTIONS: For about half the price, you can stay at one of Terme di Saturnia's sister properties (both included in the main Web site) and get free use of the spa's pools: **Saturnia Country Club,** an 18-room farmhouse a mile or so away on a 3,000-acre estate, with horseback riding, lake fishing, archery, a pool, and a restaurant (Loc. Pomonte, 58054 Scansano [GR], tel. 0564/599188, fax 0564/599214; 90,000 lire/person with breakfast); and, steps from the spa, **La Stellata Hotel,** a farmhouse with 14 rooms and a restaurant (Loc. Pian del Bagno, 58050 Saturnia [GR], tel. 0564/602978, fax 0564/602934; 135,000 lire/person half-board only). Or stay anywhere you like and pay $15 for **day use** of the spa's pools, changing rooms, showers, and sunbathing lawn. Based near Saturnia is **Maremma Mongolfiera,** offering hot-air balloon rides over the Maremma (*see* UP, UP, AND AWAY).

TORRE LE CANNELLE, NEAR TALAMONE (5L)

Where Sky Melts into Sea, p.38

Club Le Cannelle, set within the Regional Park of the Maremma, is about 2 miles from Talamone, a little walled village with a restored 14th-century fortress on a promontory above the sea. Set off by itself on its own cliff 3 miles from anything but trees (the club's rocky beach is a very long walk or short drive away) is the round tower (a 20th-century re-creation), with a kitchenette and a living room with a large wood-burning fireplace on the first floor, three bedrooms and two baths on the second and third, and the glassed-in topdeck. When gazing into even such beautiful space and wandering in your own private wilderness aren't enough, boat excursions and driving tours of coastal spots like the park, Monte Argentario, and Porto Ercole round out the time with activity. (Note: The tower is not suitable for children, and you'll need a four-wheel drive vehicle to get to and from it.)

CONTACT: Azienda Agricola Club Le Cannelle, Parco Regionale della Maremma, 58010 Talamone (GR), tel. 0564/887020, fax 0564/870470, e-mail: gitavnet@tin.it. Fishing, boat tours (May–Sept.): Pescaturismo, tel. 0564/887317, cell 0330/272278, www.agriturismo.net/pescaturismo/english.html.

DISTANCES: 200 mi from Florence, 50 mi from Siena, 93 mi from Rome.

FACILITIES: 1 tower with 3 bedrooms, 2 baths, and kitchenette. (Other accommodations are available on the property, miles from the tower, including cottages and rooms by the sea.) Horseback riding, beach.

PRICES: July–Aug., 3,000,000 lire/wk; Apr.–June, Sept., 1,800,000 lire/wk; if available, 500,000 lire/day for a 3-night minimum; no credit cards. Closed Oct.–Mar.

MAREMMA HIGHLIGHTS

Sovana (8K), Etruscan hill town built on tufa, with a major necropolis and miles of *vie cave,* sunken roads dug many feet into the tufa for purposes that remain a mystery. **Sorano,** (8K) another tufa-hilltop town, partly derelict now but with real medieval ambience and a well-preserved Renaissance fortress. **Monte Argentario** (5-6 L-M), a peninsula of rocky peaks covered with forest and macchia and sprinkled with Roman villa ruins. The attractive fishing village/resort of **Porto Ercole** (6M), with a harbor full of yachts and a colorful fish market when the boats return at sunset with shellfish, sardines, anchovies, mackerel (*caldaro,* a fish soup, is a local specialty). **Massa Maríttima** (4I), an important town of the Sienese Republic, now a lively place of shops and restaurants with a harmonious central square of *palazzi* surrounding a Pisan Romanesque cathedral and a Gothic bell tower.

SAN GIMIGNANO

Passing under the arch of San Gimignano's 13th-century Porta di San Giovanni, a monumental stone gate topped with a lookout tower, several things register at once: the splendidly preserved medieval buildings that line the narrow street; the stuffed boars that stand, hang, or pose in chef's toques outside shops selling sausage, jelly, and everything else made from the critters; and finally, unless you've timed your visit just right, the crowds. Recognized universally as one of Tuscany's wonders, the town is on the itinerary of every bus tour on its way between Florence and Siena. But make your peace with that and you will be rewarded with an eminently wanderable place of pure architecture, exciting art, and grand surprises—like the row of 10 Gothic- and Romanesque-arched public fountains built into the city walls around 1100, used later to wash fleeces for a flourishing wool trade. If you stay the night, you'll only have to share the place with the locals as little lights projecting from the stone façades illuminate the ancient squares and towers with a fairy glow, pointing the way to *trattorie* where Vernaccia di San Gimignano—exported since the 13th century, favored by Medici, and Italy's first DOC wine—is the house white.

FATTORIA POGGIO ALLORO, NEAR SAN GIMIGNANO (5F)

A Harvest Home, p.42

Fall is a great time to be in Tuscany, with celebrations everywhere starring the local vintages and markets burgeoning with fresh mushrooms (*funghi*) and black and white truffles (*tartufi*). Harvest begins toward the end of September and continues for two to four weeks. Poggio Alloro is almost an anachronism in Tuscany: a simple family farm that does it all—not just grapes and olives, but vegetables, grain, honey, chickens, pigs, rabbits, pigeons, and the famous Chianina cattle as well. And all of it ends up at the table in course after course, from *bruschetta* to *bistecca* (served once a week, usually on Saturday). It's the dinners you'll remember most, both for their bounty and for the warmth of your host and the other (mostly German) guests: getting to know them the first night, then checking in the next to see how their day's itinerary has worked out and what's up for the next. (The free-flowing spirits *do* speed familiarity.) San Gimignano is 3 miles away by car, 2 by foot on a white road through the fields past the pond.

CONTACT: Fattoria Poggio Alloro, Loc. S. Andrea, 53037 San Gimignano (SI), tel. 0577/950153 or 0577/950276, fax 0577/950290.

DISTANCES: 22 mi from Florence, 25 mi from Siena, 161 mi from Rome.

FACILITIES: 4 doubles, 2 apts. with kitchens, very simple and unadorned; 4 larger, rustic rooms in another building with stone walls and original wood-beam ceiling (along with an outdoor dining terrace facing San Gimignano) are planned for late 1999. Breakfast and dinner available. Lake for fishing only. Horseback riding at adjacent farm.

PRICES: double 90,000 lire, apt. 105,000 lire. Dinner 35,000–55,000 lire.

HOTEL LA CISTERNA (5F)

City of Towers, p.52

The Piazza della Cisterna, the smaller of San Gimignano's two main squares, is edged in adjoining towers and palazzi, one of which is now the Hotel La Cisterna. Its 14th-century façade, which makes a cameo in the 1991 film of Forster's *Where Angels Fear to Tread,* drips with vines that blaze red in autumn. Rooms at the front (as well as the first-floor reading room, all soft pink brick columns and arches, with burgundy leather couches and a windowed arched loggia) look onto the eponymous well, still imprinted with grooves from the ropes with which horses pulled up the bucket, but the stars are the four that share the (divided) tower-view terrace. The decor is merely comfortable, and rooms are a bit small, but with a terrace like this, who cares?

CONTACT: Hotel La Cisterna, Piazza della Cisterna 24, 53037 San Gimignano (SI), tel. 0577/940328, fax 0577/942080, e-mail: lacisterna@iol.it. Great Web site on the city: www.sangimignano.com.

DISTANCES: 22 mi from Florence, 30 mi from Siena, 186 mi from Rome.

FACILITIES: 47 rooms, 2 suites, with phone, safe, satellite TV, hairdryer. Restaurant serving Tuscan cuisine, with wood-beam-and-terracotta roof and window walls overlooking the valley.

PRICES: single 95,000–118,000 lire, double 140,000–195,000 lire, jr. suite 170,000–220,000 lire, including breakfast (double with balcony 170,000–195,000 lire). Closed early Jan.–early Mar.

OPTIONS: For a spectacular, horizon-filling view of the Val d'Elsa, reserve one of the 2 junior suites that have private terraces with flower boxes and iron balustrades at **Bel Soggiorno;** the restaurant, with a window wall that shares the same view, serves "specialties from Etruscan medieval kitchens." Via San Giovanni 91, 53037 San Gimignano (SI), tel. 0577/940375, fax 0577/940375, e-mail: pescille@eol.it; 150,000–220,000 lire; closed mid-Jan.–mid-Feb. Built into the town wall is a nicely appointed 2-bedroom apt. with a large roof terrace, overlooking roof gardens and several towers, that has the same valley view as Bel Soggiorno; inside are cotto floors, brick arches, and a full kitchen and dining room. **Carla Rossi,** Via di Cellole 81, 53037 San Gimignano (SI), tel. 0577/955041, cell 0368/3523206, fax 0577/941268; 140,000 lire for 2, discounts for longer stays. In several rooms at the **Hotel L'Antico Pozzo,** set in a Renaissance townhouse, the view is of Pompeii-wispy 17th-century frescoes of nymphs, garlands, and angels on walls and ceiling; rooms are gently furnished with antiques, some canopy beds, and lots of amenities. Via S. Matteo 87, 53037 San Gimignano (SI), tel. 0577/942014, fax 0577/942117, e-mail: info@anticopozzo.com, www.anticopozzo.com; double 200,000–250,000 lire, including breakfast; closed mid-Jan.–mid-Feb.

SAN GIMIGNANO HIGHLIGHTS

The Romanesque **Collegiata,** with walls covered in wondrous 15th-century frescoes by Benozzo Gozzoli (a student of Fra Angelico) and Taddeo di Bartolo, and a chapel elegantly frescoed by Ghirlandaio in tribute to Santa Fina, a devout local girl who died at 15 after years in bed, attended by miracles, becoming one of the town's patron saints. A 17-fresco cycle by Gozzoli (whose masterwork is in the Medici-Riccardi palace in Florence) in the choir of **Sant'Agostino** on the life of St. Augustine. The view of town and country from **Torre Grossa,** the town's highest tower, or from the only surviving tower of the **Fortress.**

SIENA

All rose-colored brick, Italian Gothic arches, and narrow, carless streets ranging over three hills, Siena is one of the world's loveliest medieval cities. Much of the credit for its preservation goes to bad fortune: In 1348 the Black Death killed off a third of the population, starting the city's decline; an 18-month siege

by the Florentines, which finished off the Republic of Siena in 1554, also left half its citizens dead, and the city too poor to rebuild. At its heart is the superb Piazza del Campo, ringed by cafés, 13th- and 14th-century *palazzi,* and the Palazzo Pubblico, with its slender, 330-foot-high bell tower. Beyond the joy of walking the shadowy streets, there's a lot of great art to be seen.

THE PALIO (6-7G)

Raw Siena, p.72

The Palio is run each July 2 and August 16. If you can't get a seat (hard to come by, at a minimum of about $120 each), make sure you're on the perimeter of the piazza, near the track, if you hope to see anything besides heads. Six trial runs start three days before, and on the eve of the Palio, the contradas hold very festive dinners at long tables in the streets and squares—ask the tourist office about getting a ticket to one. Reserve lodgings many months in advance.

CONTACT: Ask the APT (Il Campo 56, 53100 Siena, tel. 0577/280551, fax 0577/270676) for a list of Palio seat sellers (try Alfredo Mazzuoli, tel. 0577/280074, fax 0335/6147506; Profumeria Paolo Mancini, tel./fax 0577/289221; Longo Cini-Chiantini, tel./fax 0577/289364), or check for cancellations a few days before if you're in town. A Web site with lots of Palio info: www.comune.siena.it.

DISTANCES: 40 mi from Florence, 140 mi from Rome.

OPTIONS: A 10-minute stroll from the Campo, the **Hotel Antica Torre** is a sweet inn squeezed out of a narrow 5th-century tower, with 8 timber-and-brick-ceilinged rooms; ask for one with a panoramic view, or at least not on the noisy street side. Via di Fieravecchia 7, 53100 Siena, tel./fax 0577/222255; double $55–$100. **The Very Private Europe of Buddy Bombard** offers prime seats for the Palio and a contrada dinner as part of a 7-day luxury balloon trip. 333 Pershing Way, West Palm Beach, FL 33401–9971, tel. 800/862–8537 or 561/837–6610, fax 561/837–6623; $7,994/person all-inclusive. Or combine the Palio with a **cooking school** (*see* COOKING WITH CLASS).

SIENA HIGHLIGHTS

In the **Museo Civico,** Simone Martini's masterpiece *Maestà* and Ambrogio Lorenzetti's famous fresco pair *Allegory of Good and Bad Government.* In the **Duomo,** the marble-mosaic floor, a marble Gothic pulpit sculpted in densely detailed relief by Nicola Pisano, and the Piccolomini Library, frescoed by Pintoricchio with scenes from the life of Pope Pius II. In the **Museo dell'Opera del Duomo,** Duccio's huge *Maestà,* one of the Siena school's best paintings. In the **Ospedale di Santa Maria della Scala**—a hospital for eight centuries, now a huge museum space—a fresco cycle by Domenico di Bartolo with lively scenes from the life of the hospital and the 15th-century city. Up 500 steps, a breathtaking view of Siena and the countryside from the **Torre del Mangia.** Fresh *panforte* (a local-specialty pastry) at **Nannini.**

VERSILIA AND THE APUAN ALPS

The drive up the coast along the Ligurian Sea is a study in contrast: To your left, the beaches of Versilia, the "Italian Riviera," stretch in an endless arc, while just a few miles to your right rises a wall of mountains with caps of gleaming white marble. Hundreds of quarries are worked throughout the Apuan Alps, a chain of steep, rocky peaks and enclosed green valleys extending north from Lucca (and laced with 200 or so underground caves). Aside from the chic resorts, the area is mostly about marble, from little church-studded hillside villages of quarrymen; to towns like Carrara, with its sculpture school, its marble-paved Piazza Alberica, and its Pisa Romanesque cathedral; and Pietrasanta, with 100 workshops where artists from all over the world have come for centuries to work with skilled artisans, surrounded by students and apprentices.

THE QUARRIES OF CARRARA, APUAN ALPS (1B-C)

Into the Marble Mountains, p.42

The **Rifugio Carrara** (1B) is one of two dozen huts or shelters scattered throughout the Natural Park of the Apuan Alps; you can hike from one to another along several varied and well-marked trails. The Campocecina viewpoint is just a 10-minute walk from the parking lot below the refuge. The best view of Michelangelo's favorite marble mountain, Monte Altissimo, whose scarred, pointed peak is still being quarried today, is from the road between Seravezza and Arni.

CONTACT: Rifugio Carrara, Campocecina, tel. 0585/841972. If no one there speaks English, try APT di Carrara, tel. 0585/844403; or APT Massa-Carrara, tel. 0585/240046, fax 0585/869015, e-mail: aptms@bicnet.it, www.bicnet.it/aptms. Park information: Centro Accoglienza Visitatori, Via C. del Greco 11, 55047 Seravezza (LU), tel. 0584/757325, fax 0584/756144.

DISTANCES: 68 mi from Florence, 118 mi from Siena, 260 mi from Rome.

FACILITIES: 35 beds, shared baths. Restaurant, bar.

PRICES: 23,000 lire/person, meal 18,000 lire.

OPTIONS: From **Rifugio Donegani** (1-2B), reached by a scenic drive past a mountain-ringed aqua lake, it is an easy 1.5-hour walk through

quarries and up to a grassy hilltop with a great view of hills, valleys, and little villages; a difficult path skirts a high rocky outcrop, paying off in more expansive views. Rte. 445 north to sign for Gramolazzo to sign for Rifugio, tel. 0583/610085; 23,000 lire/person; closed Dec.–Apr. Starting at **Resceto** (2C), it's a 2.5-hour vertical walk up a mountain along the zigzagging Via Vandelli—built in the 18th century to join Massa and Modena on a marriage between the ruling houses of the two states—past chestnut woods and Roman and modern quarries to the 24-bed **Rifugio Nello Conti** (2B) and panoramic views. Campaniletti, Massa, tel. 0585/793059; 23,000 lire/person; closed wkdays mid-Sept.–May. English-speaking **park guides** are available for 190,000 lire/day for up to 25 persons; arrange it 2–3 days ahead (*see* above).

CARNEVALE, VIAREGGIO, VERSILIA (2D)

Mardi Gras, Tuscan Style, p.28

Except for breaks during the wars, Viareggio's Carnivale has been held continuously since it started in 1873 as a parade of decorated coaches filled with flowers. There are float parades (with about 14 carri, 13 masked groups, and several solos) on four consecutive Jan.–Feb. Sundays around Fat Tuesday (Martedì Grasso), when a street carnival with free events goes on all day (Carlos Santana performed in 1998, as did the usual complement of carnival bands from all over Europe); an opening ceremony and fireworks the first Saturday; and more fireworks the last Sunday, when the float prizes are awarded. (The first and last Sundays are the best.) The celebrating goes on all weekend, starting with Friday-night *rioni* (feasts) in the streets and featuring masquerades, masked balls, "vernacular comedies," sporting events, even a beauty contest. Besides the roof terrace, the Palace has front rooms with big windows the floats pass under (book one at least a month in advance), or spring for beautiful new rooms with Carrara marble-and-glass baths (with Jacuzzi), large private balconies, rich fabrics, and fine wood floors.

CONTACT: Fondazione Carnevale di Viareggio, Piazza Mazzini 22, 55049 Viareggio (LU), tel. 0584/962568, fax 0584/47077, www.viareggio.ilcarnevale.com. Palace Hotel: Lungomare ang. Via Flavio Gioia 2, 55049 Viareggio (LU), tel. 0584/46134 or 800/447-7462, fax 0584/47351, e-mail: hpalace@versilia.net, web.tin.it/palace.

DISTANCES: 57 mi from Florence, 72 mi from Siena, 232 mi from Rome.

FACILITIES: 66 rooms, 3 suites, 5 jr. suites, 2 apts., with direct-dial phone, TV. 2 restaurants, bar, rooftop bar.

PRICES: double 240,000–300,000 lire, junior suite 400,000 lire, suite 700,000 lire, including breakfast buffet.

OPTIONS: You can easily combine a Carnevale day with a stay in **Lucca,** a half-hour away (*see* LA DOLCE VITA), since special train services operate between the two towns each Sunday of Carnevale.

VERSILIA AND THE APUAN ALPS HIGHLIGHTS

Carrara's (1C) **Marble Museum,** with more than 300 highly polished slabs of marbles from all over the world, in every color and pattern, plus historical photographs, exhibits of tools, sculptures, industrial uses. **Lago di Massaciuccoli** (2D), edged in pine woods and a wetlands area that is home to 250 migratory and nesting bird species, including night, blue-gray, and purple herons. **Torre del Lago** (2D), the palm-accented lakeside hamlet where Puccini lived and wrote most of his masterpieces, with boat tours, his house museum (with a chapel in which he was buried), and an open-air stage and 4,000-seat grandstand where the Puccini Festival is held each summer. **Grotta del Vento** (2C), the "Wind Cave," with guided tours through wide lighted tunnels filled with interesting stalagmites and stalactites.

Photographer Antonio Sferlazzo, a native and spiritual son of the Maremma, who is largely responsible for the choice of locations in this book, lives in the countryside outside Florence, tending his garden. Innovative and painterly in its portrayals of landscapes, his work has appeared both in Italy and the United States in exhibitions and in major magazines, including *l'Espresso, Gourmet, European Travel and Life,* and *GQ*. In 1993 *Aperture* included his images in its prestigious monograph on Italian photographers, which accompanied a traveling show that debuted at the Guggenheim Foundation in Venice and was exhibited in New York at the Murray and Isabella Rayburn Foundation.

Author Candice Gianetti, a longtime freelance writer and editor, fell in love with Italy unexpectedly during a brief visit cobbled onto the end of a long Greek idyll. Back then, when she hit Florence, she was immediately afflicted by a malady of romantic 19th-century travelers known as the Stendhal Syndrome, after the French novelist who was so affected by the glories of the city that he walked "in constant fear of falling to the ground." Even after months of work on this book, she still feels the same way.